IT'S ALL TOO MUCH

Adventures of a Teenage Beatles Fan in the '60s and Beyond

David Stark

THIS DAY
IN MUSIC BOOKS
thisdayinmusicbooks.com

This edition © This Day In Music Books 2020
Text © This Day In Music Books / David Stark
By arrangement with SongLink International

ISBN 978-1-8380708-1-6 Paperback Edition
ISBN 978-1-8380708-2-3 Digital Edition

Front cover artwork by Ingrid Black
www.ingridblack.com
Front cover layout by Paul Endacott
Index and proofing by Malcolm Wyatt
Book Design by Gary Bishop
Printed in the UK by Sound Performance

THIS DAY IN MUSIC BOOKS

This Day In Music Books
2B Vantage Park
Washingley Road
Huntingdon
PE29 6SR

www.thisdayinmusic.com

For
John, Paul, George and Ringo;
Everyone who knows me and
all Beatles fans worldwide.

"Entertaining, celebrating, meditating years
The greatest show on earth for all to hear..."

(From 'Gold Songs' by Fab Gear)

∞℘

ALSO BY DAVID STARK

INSPIRATIONS: Original Lyrics and the
Stories Behind the Greatest Songs Ever Written

(With Mike Read and Michael Randolfi, 1999)

CONTENTS

FOREWORD #1

It was at the National Film Theatre in 1981, just a few months after John Lennon's murder, that I was introduced to David Stark by our mutual friend Mark Lewisohn.

"You've got to meet this guy," Mark had told me. "He's had these *amazing* encounters with The Beatles ..."

"Such as?"

"Such as sitting directly behind them at the *Yellow Submarine* premiere."

Okay, not many people had done *that*.

"He also gatecrashed the *Magic Christian* premiere, saw a couple of their concerts, was in the audience for *The Rolling Stones Rock and Roll Circus* ..."

Yep, I had to meet this guy. And Dave didn't disappoint when we three hooked up at the NFT — regaling us with some of the stories that appear within these pages.

"Here's a photo of me with John at the Selfridges book signing ... and one with George outside Capital Radio ..."

He also had a copy of the recently-published Ray Connolly book, *John Lennon 1940-1980*, containing a pic of John and Yoko about to enter Marylebone Magistrates Court following their pot bust ... trailed closely by a young chappie, then just 15-years-old, who was instantly recognisable as the one now sitting opposite me.

The word that sprang to mind as Dave spoke was *chutzpah*. Even as a kid, he already had the inclination, smarts and sheer bloody nerve to do the kinds of things the rest of us wish we'd done too. Yet, he never boasted; he just shared his adventures — which continued after we became fast friends.

"He's a nice guy," another mate of mine commented one night after Dave phoned to say he'd been chatting with Paul McCartney at some press event. "But how can you be sure he's telling the truth with all these stories?"

The answer arrived a short time later when Dave dropped by with a paparazzi pic of him, wine glass in hand, standing next to Macca.

The photos kept coming with each new escapade — as well as some from the past.

"Bloody hell, take a look at page 40," he said over the phone after my interview with him for the 20th anniversary of the *Yellow Submarine* premiere was published in *The Beatles Book* magazine. There, standing behind George in the lobby of the London Pavilion, was young Dave. He'd never seen that pic before;

the first solid evidence — followed several years later by film footage of him approaching George at the same event.

The Beatles Zelig — time after time, he was *thur*, as George would say, as well as *hur* and every-bloody-*whur*. What's more, he has an incredible memory — for faces, as well as for the names and events associated with them. Many times I've seen Dave recognise people from brief encounters who clearly don't recognise him —and watched their scepticism turn to amazement as he's recounted in precise detail the circumstances in which they met many years before.

That kind of recall is invaluable for a storyteller — as is his uncanny ability to always deliver the goods. Once, after he'd returned from a trip to Cuba, I facetiously asked Dave if he'd run into Fidel Castro. That was like asking a visitor to the UK if he or she had bumped into the Queen. Dave, of course, said he had indeed met and spoken with Fidel, before — just as predictably — showing me the photographic proof.

This, for me, is just another example of why the name David Stark is synonymous with fascinating anecdotes about legendary characters — and why I'm so glad he's finally written this book: filled with his up-close insights, laced with his humour. I just hope he's now working on a second volume comprising all of his non-Beatles-related stories.

Richard Buskin, Chicago, USA
September 2020
www.richardbuskin.com

FOREWORD #2

I met David Stark during what feels like a hundred years ago, in some dark, dilapidated dive the other side of reality. I must have done. There was a time when I spent my life in such places. I had worked in music and showbiz media for many years by then. Our paths would have crossed on numerous occasions in the moonlight, only to trail inconclusively beyond the dawn. It struck me much later that our first encounter, if only I could remember the when, the where and the why of it, had a similar effect to that of buying a new car: one may never before have noticed a Suzuki Jeep or a Volkswagen Polo, say, until the moment one acquired one's own. After that, they are everywhere.

All roads, contacts and requests suddenly led to David Stark. In another life, he'd have been a Gene Kilroy, Muhammad Ali's right-hand man known as 'the Facilitator'; or an unassuming, male version of *Hello!* magazine's Marquesa de Varela, who has interviewed, bigged up, played down, helped and remained pals with 'absolutely everyone'. Close friend, confidant, ally, fixer. The guy who always has time for the guy or gal who needs something; whose favour bank is heaving with favours due.

David writes here about 'chutzpah' and 'sheer luck' having led him into his astonishing life in music. Yeah, right. Don't be deceived by his humility. The schoolboy Beatles fan who inveigled his way into countless celebrity situations he had no legitimate business being at was pointedly determined. There is no 'right place, right time' to this. None of that 'chance' nonsense. Stark knew what he was doing. He knows still.

When I decided, in 2018, to write a book about John Lennon in commemoration of the fortieth anniversary of his assassination and what would have been his 80th birthday, both of which fell in 2020, David did not hesitate. Not only did he share with me his recorded interview with Pete Shotton, John's lifelong best friend since the age of six, which had never been published. He also fixed it for me to accompany him to the 2019 summer Graduation Day at the Liverpool Institute of Performing Arts (LIPA), where I was lucky enough to converse at length with Sir Paul McCartney. David also shared reminiscences of days spent with John's Aunt Mimi, the woman who brought Lennon up. The pictures tell the tale. Thanks to 'D.S.', they are also in my book. No one did more to help me piece together the intricacies of John's life. 'Grateful' is too flimsy a word, but you get me.

His Fab Four recollections are the very best kind of first-hand tales. The childhood that led to his obsession with John, Paul, George and Ringo and to all those other artists and bands, endless bands, many of whom are now his personal friends, reveals what a foregone conclusion his life path has been. He writes simply and disarmingly, with genuine wonder at where Fate has led him. You will find not one boastful syllable here. He is still amazed. His enthusiasm knows no bounds. I think you will love this book.

Lesley-Ann Jones, September 2020
Author, 'Who Killed John Lennon? The Lives,
Loves and Deaths of the Greatest Rock Star'
www.lesleyannjones.com

PREFACE

July 17, 1968

The cinema lights stayed on for a few minutes, as I quickly got my bearings, looked around and took in the enormity of the occasion. Seated to my immediate right, clad in a dark velvet jacket, was the legendary wasted rock star guitarist, who casually informed me that it was cool to sit next to him, as his rubber-lipped bandmate was away in New York with his blonde singer girlfriend.

So they wouldn't be needing the two empty aisle seats in the second row; a big surprise but highly welcome news indeed. Immediately in front of me, in the front row, was the back of one of the most famous heads in the world, whose owner was engaged in conversation with an attractive reddish-blonde haired girl to his left. I didn't quite recognise her, but knew she wasn't his close partner of the past few years, with whom he'd just broken up.

To his immediate right was his boyhood pal and songwriting partner, wearing his usual National Health-style rounded spectacles, and sporting an eye-catching white suit with a black shirt. Sitting on his right was his new Japanese partner, still a bit of a mystery lady, who'd never been seen with him at such a major event before.

Alongside her were the other two members of the famous foursome with their wives, all colourfully dressed for the occasion. Suddenly, the lights began to dim, while the celebrity-laden audience slowly started to hush. My heart was pounding fast, in case anyone would possibly still come to eject my friend and I from the centre-row aisle seats we'd just been given permission to occupy.

It was hard to believe that, a little under 30 minutes earlier, we had been standing — for some time — on the roof of the former Victorian theatre we were now sitting in. And that, quite incredibly, we were now occupying two celebrity seats in the dress circle of the London Pavilion cinema on Piccadilly Circus. The event that evening was the world premiere of The Beatles' highly anticipated animated film, *Yellow Submarine*, and I was there, right behind the group themselves.

Thanks to a combination of sheer luck and chutzpah, just minutes earlier, I'd managed to secure official approval for us both to stay for this huge showbiz occasion, despite a lack of any formal invitation. And now, courtesy of Keith Richards of the Rolling Stones, I was — most astonishingly — sitting directly behind John, Paul, George and Ringo, on a night which would later turn out to be London's last outpouring of mass Beatlemania.

Talk about good fortune: I'd somehow landed in the heart of pop music's royal epicentre, when London was still very much swinging in the music, film, art and fashion departments. Even if only for a couple of hours, it was a dream come true for this 15-year old schoolboy and huge Beatles fan.

*

July 28, 2006

Fast-forward 38 years and I'm standing behind a lectern, on stage at Liverpool's Philharmonic Hall. I was about to deliver a speech to around 200 students, graduating that day from LIPA, the Liverpool Institute for Performing Arts. In the audience were their parents and families; many local dignitaries and other honoured guests.

Plus, Sir Paul McCartney, the founding Patron of LIPA, sitting centre-stage in the historic concert hall, known locally as 'The Philly', where his own school prize ceremonies were held during the 1950s, as he'd mention later. But for now, he was sitting in the seat next to the one I'd just vacated on stage, and about to listen to what I had to say.

Once again, my heart was beating as I began explaining to Paul, the other guests and dignitaries; and all the graduating students, dressed in their mortarboards and gowns, how The Beatles had influenced my life and choice of career in the music industry. I related how the group's incredible impact on me from a very early age had led to this special day, on which I was being honoured as a 'Companion of LIPA' for my work with songwriter students at the highly-acclaimed facility.

As I looked around the crowded hall, I briefly found myself wondering how on earth this had all come about ...

CHAPTER 1

IN THE TOWN WHERE I WAS BORN

As families go, ours was fairly typical of the reasonably well-to-do, post-war generation of north-west London, where we lived in a mock-Tudor detached house in Stanmore, the last stop on the Bakerloo line. Our family consisted of Mum and Dad, myself and my brother Nigel, two and a half years younger than me. Our house wasn't huge, quite modest in fact, but in a pleasant street with friendly neighbours. As small boys in the 1950s, Nigel and I spent much of our time in the morning room, where we usually ate our meals, and where our toy cupboard was located beneath some crockery and linen shelves. Over time, that lower cupboard section became ever more crammed, with our most dreaded parental instruction jokily being,

"Tidy your toys up now boys, or we'll take them away from you."

Our parents, Norman and Kathy, aged 40 and 34 respectively in 1959, were a good-looking couple who always stood out in photos and home movies. Mum was extremely pretty, tall and slim with dark hair, striking features and always beautifully turned-out, with a great feel for the right clothes and hats. So much so, that during the mid-'60s, she decided to become an independent fashion consultant, which didn't last long but did result in her being photographed for the Daily Mirror.

Dad had a somewhat different persona, having been a dashing young man in his twenties, driving an eye-catching Jaguar and being a bit of a hit with the ladies. However, we knew him more as a slightly eccentric character with some increasingly noticeable OCD tendencies over the years. Everything had to stay exactly in its place; 'You mustn't touch this or that', and, 'You boys must put on your (identical) blue suits for shul (synagogue).' Plus, he was something of a hypochondriac who had a history of illnesses, both physical and mental, which later led to a severe nervous breakdown. But to be fair, Dad always tried to do his best for us, although there were often some rather heated exchanges along the way.

Mum, on the other hand, was extremely easy-going, kind and gentle with a soft, soothing voice. She was also a very good cook, whose most popular dishes enjoyed by us included roast chicken, beef and lamb, meatballs, shepherd's pie and fried or gefilte fish. As Nigel and I grew older, we were eventually allowed to have our supper in the dining room, mainly on Friday nights, the start of the Jewish sabbath. Mum took this reasonably seriously by lighting the traditional candles and saying a blessing, although we were far from being orthodox in the religion department.

As many relations and friends often said, Nigel looked more like Dad and had also inherited his interest in cars, mechanics and anything electrical; while I took after Mum's more artistic sensibilities, as well as her brown eyes and facial features. Their two boisterous sons usually looked fairly presentable — until certain incidents happened, such as Nigel ripping his new suit jacket on the front gate, and getting his pure white top covered in thick black creosote in the garden shed.

I also suffered an unfortunate accident at an early age, when I crashed my tricycle into an extremely flash car owned by one of our neighbours, by the name of Jimmy Jacobs. Luckily, he was extremely nice about the incident, telling Mum, Dad and little me not to worry about it, and not asking for a penny in damages. Little did I know then that he co-owned Soho's most infamous striptease club, The Gargoyle in Dean Street, which was where the equally notorious Nell Gwyn, actress and mistress to King Charles II, had reportedly lived in a long-gone house on the site during the 17th century.

Speaking of history, Mum's maiden name was Mendoza, with her ancestors being Sephardic Jews who originated from Cordoba and Seville in Spain, expelled by law from the country in 1609. Most of the Jewish community made their way to Belgium and the Netherlands, before some were allowed entry into England during the 1650s — but only after Oliver Cromwell relaxed the country's strict immigration and religious laws.

Mum's most celebrated ancestor was the bare-knuckle boxer Daniel Mendoza, born in 1764, who became the most accomplished fighter of his time, a master of ring strategy and defence. He was the champion boxer of England from 1790-92, but despite his fame and prize-fighting success he was later found guilty of fraud, due to his lack of business acumen, serving time for his crime in debtors' prison.

However, 'Mendoza the Jew' did revolutionise self-defence in the sport, helped by publication of his widely-acclaimed book *The Art of Boxing,* subsequently becoming a much-admired figure who also helped elevate the status of Jews in London at that time. He died in 1836 at the age of 72, leaving 11 children and many grandchildren, and was buried in the East End before being reburied in Brentwood Jewish Cemetery, near to where Nigel lives today.

The Mendoza clan in London grew rapidly over the next 100 years, with its most famous son born in 1925, the same year as Mum. He was the actor Peter Sellers, whose mother, Agnes Doreen Marks (aka 'Peg'), was descended from the Mendoza family, while her Yorkshire-born husband Bill was Protestant. Both were variety entertainers in the 1920s, with Peg being a singer and Bill a pianist.

Peter Sellers was extremely proud of his heritage, even placing framed portraits of Daniel Mendoza in background shots of some of his films. Virtually every biography on Sellers mentions Mendoza in its early chapters, while there have also been plays and short films made about the celebrated pugilist. I own a few books about him, and years ago researched his story at the British Library, where I discovered some fascinating original manuscripts related to his life and career.

In the late 1970s, I was friendly with Peter's son, Michael Sellers, a cousin who became a carpenter by trade, but who also had strong musical leanings. His father originally played the drums, as I do, while Michael was into guitars. We formed a rather short-lived band, rehearsing in the garage of his mother Anne's Hampstead home, located in the next street to where I now live. We reconnected many years later at a tribute dinner to his father, but tragically Michael died in 2006, from the same cause, a heart attack; at the same age, just 54; and on exactly the same date, July 24, as his father's death in 1980. An extraordinarily sad triple coincidence.

*

I was born on October 26, 1952 in the St. David's wing of the now-demolished Royal Northern Hospital in Holloway Road, north London. It's worth mentioning here that 1952 was also the year which marked the inception of three very different and long-running institutions, which are all still with us today at the time of writing. Well almost, thanks to one slight exception caused by Coronavirus.

Firstly, H.M. Queen Elizabeth II inherited the throne on February 6, 1952, upon the death of her father George VI. Although uncrowned, she was already Queen when I was born, and is now nearing a quite remarkable 70 years of rule. I've never been fortunate enough to meet Her Majesty (as yet) but have seen her in public on a few occasions and taken a photograph or two of her.

Secondly, Agatha Christie's celebrated play *The Mousetrap* originally opened in Nottingham on October 6, 1952, just 20 days before I was born. It then went on tour before beginning its London run on November 25, 1952 at the Ambassadors Theatre, transferring to the larger St Martin's Theatre in 1974. I've only seen it once, many years ago, but in recent years have become an avid Agatha Christie fan, reading many of her books and watching the old Poirot series on television during lockdown. The play was all set to reopen in October 2020, for which I'd booked tickets around our mutual 68th birthdays, but sadly this has since been postponed until 2021 due to that cursed virus.

The third, and most personally relevant, fact about my birth year is that the first-ever British record chart was published in the *New Musical Express* on November 14, 1952. That chart was a Top 12 aggregated from phone calls made to just 20 record shops, with Al Martino's 'Here in My Heart' achieving the first-ever Number One position. Other artists on the list included Nat King Cole, Bing Crosby, Doris Day, Frankie Laine, Max Bygraves and the late great Vera Lynn (two entries). I would very much like to have informed you which record was at Number One on the day I was born, but by Sod's law there was no British pop chart for another three weeks.

It took a little more than 10 years before the charts would hold any real significance in my early life. To be precise, it was in January 1963 when I first became aware of a certain northern England beat combo hailing from Liverpool.

Before then, it was songs like 'Nellie The Elephant' by Mandy Miller; 'The Runaway Train' by Michael Holliday; and 'The Ugly Duckling' by Danny Kaye, all of which Nigel and I loved listening to as kids in the late '50s. As well as hearing them played regularly on the BBC's *Children's Favourites* radio programme on Saturday mornings, presented by Derek McCulloch aka 'Uncle Mac', we also had 78rpm versions of some of these records at home, as bought by Mum and Dad.

We loved playing the brittle 10-inch discs on Nigel's vintage wind-up record-player, given to him as a present, along with others like 'The Bee Song' by Arthur Askey, 'I Taut I Taw a Puddy Tat' (Mel Blanc), 'Sparky's Magic Piano' (Henry Blair) and 'They're Changing Guards at Buckingham Palace' (Ann Stephens). That was, until we eventually discovered the dubious pleasure of using the records as prototype frisbees, ending up smashing many of the precious discs upstairs in the attic, where our parents couldn't hear us. Sacrilege indeed.

Luckily, the much sturdier 45rpm vinyl singles were a lot harder to break, and I still have my copy of the first one I ever bought at the age of eight in March 1961: the King Brothers' hit version of 'Seventy-Six Trombones', released on EMI's Parlophone label. Unbeknown to me then, within a couple of years that familiar imprint with the pound-sign logo was to become an extremely important addition to my small record collection.

Meanwhile my favourite pop artists in the early '60s included Cliff Richard and the Shadows, Adam Faith, Anthony Newley, Chubby Checker and Frank Ifield (you remember him), along with an exotic-looking dark-haired teenage female. The siren from Stepney, aka Helen Shapiro, was a nice Jewish girl from East London with a deep resonant voice, who definitely wobbled the collies of this young fan whenever I saw her on TV. Years later, I would meet and dine with her, as she became a good friend of my step-sister Deborah and family, with whom she shares religious beliefs.

However, there was another pop sound which, as mentioned, suddenly hit me for six in early 1963, during one of the coldest winters on record when snow covered most of the country, and didn't start thawing until March. I still remember the precise moment when I heard that upcoming Liverpool beat combo for the very first time: I was standing at the foot of the stairs in our lounge hall, aged just 10 and listening to a vibrant new record on the radio which featured a memorable harmonica intro, unique-sounding harmonies and an overall energy which just captivated me on the spot.

It was shortly before five o'clock on that wintry Sunday afternoon in January, when Alan 'Fluff' Freeman announced a record climbing the nation's charts during his weekly *Pick of the Pops* show on the BBC's Light Programme. The song was titled 'Please Please Me', as recorded by a group curiously named 'The Beatles'. Upon hearing it, my young world was suddenly transformed for life.

I was completely overwhelmed by this exciting new sound: I'd never heard anything like it before, and neither had the majority of the British public. However, it wasn't too long before everyone knew exactly who these rather striking, long-haired Beatles from Merseyside were: John, Paul, George and Ringo, a group which had its own distinctive style; great senses of humour; wrote many of their own songs and suddenly looked like the coolest four young men on the planet.

I couldn't get enough of them on radio, television or in the press, so much so that within a short time I started to keep an eye out for anything to do with them in the papers and stuck the cuttings in the first of my many Beatles scrapbooks. I followed their every move as much as I could, from concerts to photo-shoots and television appearances to overseas tours, building up a sizeable collection of press cuttings and photographs from very early on, which still make for fascinating reading.

Within a short period of time, the incredible 'Fab Four' seemed to be everywhere, and my conversion was complete. From then on, it was goodbye, or at least *au revoir* to Cliff, the Shadows and even Helen, as The Beatles quickly became the new kings of pop, reigning supreme from then on.

'Please Please Me' was followed in April 1963 by 'From Me To You' before the group's two huge super-smashes were released later that year. 'She Loves You' was issued in September and 'I Want To Hold Your Hand' in late November, the latter rounding off Christmas and the New Year for five weeks at No. 1. However, it was 'She Loves You', with Ringo's iconic opening drum roll; its anthemic 'Yeah, yeah, yeah' chorus with such memorable harmonies; and just being such an exuberant and game-changing record, which confirmed The Beatles' much-deserved acclaim to me as the best band in the land.

Nigel and I loved the B-sides as much as the A-sides, especially 'I'll Get You', the flip-side of 'She Loves You', with its catchy *'Oh yeah'* refrain, while the flip of 'I Want To Hold Your Hand' was the haunting ballad 'This Boy', with its immaculately-sung harmonies. Indeed, this Beatle-mad schoolboy, now all of 11 years old, was totally obsessed with the group, despite Dad's insistence to me at the time that...

"These Beatles will never last."

Er, thanks Dad, just stick to the shmutter business, okay. Dad had worked all his life along with younger brother Kenneth at the family garment business, H.

Stark (aka Hi-Star), located in Dalston, east London. The factory specialised in making 'Civilian and Military Clothing' and was founded by their father, Hyman Stark, whose story was classic Jewish immigrant-made-good in the early twentieth century. Actually, rather better than good, as my grandfather became a highly respected philanthropist who later helped found the Regent's Park Open Air Theatre among other worthwhile endeavours. At one point, years before, he supposedly had a share in all the public conveniences in Paris, according to family legend. I suppose he felt rather flush at the time if true.

Meanwhile, Dad was an expert cutter and tailor, but also an outstanding amateur electrician who built his own radio sets and even televisions as a young man in the 1930s; knew cars inside out; and had installed our home central heating system by himself. In another life he could have easily become an electronics (or plumbing) magnate, but instead worked long hours at the factory, commuting each day.

In September 1948 he married Kathleen Mendoza of Hendon, youngest of four children to Sydney and Rae Mendoza. Mum could have possibly been on the stage if her father had allowed her to go to RADA acting school, as did one of her school alumni, Jean Simmons, who did indeed become a famous screen actress. Nevertheless, Mum did work for ENSA during the war, helping send theatrical artistes to entertain the troops at various locations. After their wedding in West Hampstead, the happy couple lived in Queensbury, near Wembley before I arrived, when we moved to Jesmond Way in suburban Stanmore.

Dad was more into Judy Garland, Frank Sinatra and other stars of the '40s and '50s. He couldn't see anything in The Beatles other than loud noise and long hair. However, Mum was a big music fan, mainly of musicals, and also appeared in a couple of shows at our local synagogue along with her good friend Claire Rayner, later of books and television fame. To give her credit, Mum was quite supportive of my craze for what she jokingly called '*pop shmop*', and put up with my constant record-playing in the lounge, as long as it wasn't too loud.

*

Later that year, I purchased my first LP record, *With The Beatles*, released on exactly the same day that President John F. Kennedy was assassinated, November 22, 1963. It was a tragedy which I still associate with watching *Ready Steady Go!* and *Take Your Pick* on ITV, just minutes before hearing the grim news from our Uncle Kenneth, who rushed over to share it with us that Friday evening. I actually went up to my bedroom to cry, years later becoming fascinated with anything to do with JFK's assassination, as I still am today. Three years later, I chose the case as the subject for my O-Level oral exam, speaking to the class about possible conspiracy theories.

With The Beatles was a superb album with an iconic sleeve, almost as important as the record itself back in those days. I would look at Robert Freeman's masterful black and white photographs of the group for ages while listening to the record, and loved all the songs, of which seven were written by Lennon and McCartney. One was by George Harrison, 'Don't Bother Me', while the rest were covers of the Marvelettes, Miracles and others, whom I knew nothing about. But it didn't matter: they were all Beatles songs as far as I was concerned. From the three classic opening tracks, 'It Won't Be Long', 'All I've Got To Do' and 'All My Loving', to Ringo's jaunty 'I Wanna Be Your Man' and John's gritty version of 'Money', I enjoyed it all, playing my sole long-player many times over on our teak-finished stereogram in the lounge.

The year 1963 eventually turned into '64, and as I noted in my Lett's Schoolboy Diary, The Beatles touched down in New York on Friday February 7 for the first time, to a tremendous reception. This was when Beatlemania truly went worldwide, and as I'd never actually seen the group in person at that time, I was more than envious of all those lucky fans across the pond getting the chance to see our home-grown pop princes up close and personal in their own backyard. I followed the tour through George's regular column in the *Daily Express*, actually written by Beatles PR man Tony Barrow, a very nice chap who I got to know years later.

At the time, I was also an avid reader of *Fabulous*, a large-format pop weekly, later renamed *Fabulous 208,* which featured giant full-colour photos of all the current chart stars. My diary also notes that, just three days after the British invasion of February 7, *Fabulous* published an 'all-Beatles Fab mag', which was like manna from heaven to my scrapbooks.

*

The summer of 1964 saw the release of The Beatles' first feature film, *A Hard Day's Night*, with my diary also revealing that Mum took Nigel and I to see it at Watford Odeon just a few days after it opened in early July. Nigel tells me we also went back to see it with Dad a few days later. And what a fabulous film it is, still looking and sounding remarkably fresh to this day, while the punchy spot-on script by Alun Owen remains quite outstanding. It was so exciting to see The Beatles on the big screen, while in my opinion, *A Hard Day's Night* is as much a British celluloid icon of the early '60s as *A Taste of Honey* or *Billy Liar,* if not more so.

The eponymous album was terrific too, being The Beatles' first and only one on which every song was written by Lennon and McCartney. It featured 13 tracks in just over 30 minutes, the seven songs on side one all featured on the film soundtrack, opening with that iconic guitar and piano chord on the title track, which continues to confound musicologists and music copyists to this day.

The album was a great mix of up-tempos and ballads, of which John's 'I Should Have Known Better' and 'If I Fell'; and Paul's 'And I Love Her' and 'Things We Said Today' were all particularly strong, along with the two monster singles, the title track and 'Can't Buy Me Love'. The album was hardly ever off our record deck that summer, not least because I couldn't actually afford to start buying records by other artists on my meagre pocket money until a couple of years later. In fact, I had a private policy of staying completely loyal to the Fab Four until 1966, with my first non-Beatles album being *A Quick One* by The Who, my second favourite group.

I had just left Aylward Primary School in Stanmore, which I had attended since 1960, and was looking forward to starting at Haberdashers' Aske's School in Elstree in the autumn of 1964. 'Habs,' as it's commonly known, was a direct grant (aka posh) school which I'd passed the entrance exam to, along with a few of my Aylward pals like Paul Levett, my oldest friend to this day. The school had a first-class reputation and was situated within acres of superb grounds in the lush Hertfordshire countryside, which meant catching a school coach every day from Stanmore tube station. If we ever missed it, we were in trouble, with 'kissing the moach' being the required euphemism for anyone unlucky enough to do so.

I quite enjoyed being at the new school, mainly thanks to a couple of excellent, if slightly eccentric, teachers in English and Art, my two favourite subjects. English teacher Simon Stuart, actually a Lord who drove an Aston Martin DB6, was an inspirational character who wrote a deeply analytical book about our second-year class, entitled *Say*, while lessons with art teacher Laurence Broderick were often hilarious, thanks to his occasional habit of conducting them from a dustbin.

Unfortunately, I couldn't quite muster up similar enthusiasm for music lessons, which I usually found quite tedious and boring, except when some jolly tunes like Prokofiev's 'Lieutenant Kijé' and others were played in class. Notable Habs' alumni like the late Chris Squire of Yes and Rick Wright of Pink Floyd, both some years older than me, might well have had the same attitude. Who knows.

*

My first encounter with anyone connected with The Beatles also occurred in that summer of '64, during a family holiday at the Imperial Hotel in Torquay, to which Dad drove us down in his year-old Humber Sceptre saloon. The hotel was one of the most popular on what's endearingly known as the 'English Riviera', and while sitting by the pool one day, Mum and Dad began chatting with a young couple named Clive and Barbara, down from Liverpool for a few days' break.

Clive Epstein was the younger brother of Beatles manager Brian and also a director of NEMS, the Epstein family company originally known as North End Music Stores. As you can imagine, I was more than excited to meet him and ask lots of questions about The Beatles, which he was happy to answer, not that I can remember any of our chat. Both he and Barbara were good company and got on well with our parents.

Clive had a noticeable resemblance to Brian but with reddish hair, and like his famous brother no hint whatsoever of any Liverpool accent. At one point, a photo was taken of the four of us and the Epsteins by the pool, a nice memento of a most unexpected encounter, if I could only find it. Before we departed, Clive promised to keep in touch. A week or so after we arrived home, I received a package sent from him at NEMS in Liverpool which contained a set of glossy black and white press photos of 'the boys', as still mounted in one of my early scrapbooks.

Four years later, dropping Clive's name was to prove a critically important godsend, during what would become my most remarkable encounter with The Beatles.

Clive Epstein in later life

CHAPTER 2

WE HOPE YOU WILL ENJOY THE SHOW

On Wednesday, January 6, 1965, as my Letts schoolboy diary proudly proclaims in large pencil-written letters, the family went to see *Another Beatles Christmas Show* at Hammersmith Odeon. This was the group's second festive offering in London, following a successful season at the Astoria in Finsbury Park the previous winter.

As I recall, Dad managed to secure the tickets through an accountant acquaintance by the name of Charles Silver, who also happened to be music publisher Dick James' silent partner in Northern Songs, the company he formed with Brian Epstein to administer The Beatles' song catalogue.

Years later, I remember Dad mentioning something about being asked to be an investor in Dick's fledgling publishing company before it was launched. However, he declined as he knew nothing whatsoever about music. I was pretty stunned to hear this, especially considering what financial returns might have been achieved on any investment, however small, in a future Beatles-related company, which eventually went public on the Stock Exchange.

So off we all went by car to Hammersmith in west London for what proved to be a quite tumultuous evening. The Odeon was for years London's largest cinema (3,487 seats), and later a famous concert venue, one I was to visit many times over the next 50-plus years. However, this was my first time there, as well as being the one and only time I ever saw The Beatles playing live in concert. Of course, it was practically impossible to hear them properly because of the constant screaming. Nevertheless, I was totally ecstatic to be there and soak in the incredible atmosphere of the occasion, despite the incessant noise, which hardly ever stopped.

Our seats were upstairs in the balcony but quite near the front. In slight confusion, we watched a sketch during the first half of the show which featured The Beatles dressed up as Antarctic explorers, searching for the Abominable Snowman. Had we been able to hear the dialogue a little clearer above the screaming, I'm sure we might have understood what it was all about, but we got the gist of it. Still, it didn't really matter, as just seeing John, Paul, George and Ringo in person, all clad in fur-lined explorer gear and mucking about on stage, was a real treat.

Other artists on the bill included Freddie & The Dreamers, Elkie Brooks, Sounds Incorporated, Mike Haslam, the Mike Cotton Sound, comedian Ray Fell, and The Yardbirds, with Eric Clapton on lead guitar. Apparently, it was during the three-week run of this Christmas show that he became friendly with George Harrison, and rare film footage in recent Clapton documentary *Life In 12 Bars* pictures the Yardbirds hanging out backstage with The Beatles. The compère for the evening was DJ Jimmy Savile, not quite as notorious in those days, Nigel having distinct memories of him jokily messing about with The Beatles' microphones before they came back on to close the second half of the show.

Their 11-song set began with 'Twist and Shout', at which point the entire audience went completely nuts, forcing Mum to put her hands over her ears with a nervous smile. I was quite overwhelmed by it all, desperately trying to hear the music but ultimately just taking in the experience of actually seeing The Beatles playing, familiar from so many TV appearances. John standing to the right with legs apart and guitar held high on his chest; Paul and George in tandem to the left, shaking their heads during every chorus; and Ringo at the back, bravely attempting to keep time despite being unable to hear much from the group's meagre amplifiers and speakers.

For the record, their full set-list consisted of 'Twist and Shout', 'I'm a Loser', 'Baby's in Black', 'Everybody's Trying To Be My Baby', 'Can't Buy Me Love', 'Honey Don't', 'I Feel Fine', 'She's a Woman', 'A Hard Day's Night', 'Rock and Roll Music' and 'Long Tall Sally'. It's all a distant memory now, but at least we were there and still have the original concert programme, with its distinctive Lennon line-drawing on the cover, portraying a festive couple, complete with holly and mistletoe.

*

So now I'd actually seen The Beatles in concert, but from then on I had to make do with just seeing them on screen as before. At least there were a few great television shows, ones I never missed, such as *Around The Beatles, Big Night Out* and *Ready Steady Go!*, screened in 1964, while in 1965 they appeared on *Thank Your Lucky Stars, Top of the Pops* and *Blackpool Night Out* along with comedians Mike and Bernie Winters, as screened on August 1.

August also saw the release of The Beatles' second film *Help!*, which my diary reminds me that I went to see with a friend on August 7 at the Odeon cinema in Burnt Oak, a 15-minute bus ride from home. It was a highly enjoyable technicolour follow-up to *A Hard Day's Night,* with a silly plot involving the search for Ringo's sacrificial ring plus a great bunch of new songs, of which John's title track was a terrific album opener (and his last until *Abbey Road* four years later).

It all brings back memories of seeing double-bill features at the cinema in those days (the main feature plus a B-movie), while watching The Beatles in such exotic locations as the Bahamas and the Austrian Alps was a lot of fun. Although the script wasn't quite as sharp as *A Hard Day's Night*, it had its moments, with the musical sequences all being very impressive. Especially 'Ticket to Ride', set in the Alps, with The Beatles in morse-code mode, along with the scene's clever use of using telegraph wires as musical staves. I also loved 'You're Gonna Lose That Girl' with its beautifully-lit shots of the group playing in the studio.

One other memorable sequence was the one in which they all walked separately through the front doors of four terraced houses, actually located in Twickenham, which turned out to be one vast single home inside. At one point, Paul can be seen playing an art deco-style organ, upon which a few *Superman, Jimmy Olsen* and *Action Comics* are sitting on the shelf where the sheet-music should be.

Nigel and I loved all those DC Comics and had a sizeable collection between us. In fact, I received every issue of *Superman* from the States each month, thanks to a pal who received two by mistake and gave me one. If only I still had them today. Many of those original '60s editions are worth a small fortune.

The release, on December 3, 1965, of the *Rubber Soul* album and double A-side single 'Day Tripper/We Can Work It Out' took The Beatles back to the top of both the singles and album charts. Commencing with Paul's clever and chirpy 'Drive My Car', it was actually the softer tracks like 'Norwegian Wood', 'Michelle' and 'Girl' which became instant classics, while John's thoughtful 'In My Life' was recognised as a very special song. Another of my favourites (and it still is) was 'The Word', with its funky piano sound, while Ringo's playing on this one and throughout the album is excellent. It was also impressive that The Beatles continued to give their fans great value for money by not including either side of the new single on it.

I was also very much struck by the album cover's ingenious title lettering, which to my art-conscious mind represented one of the earliest examples of psychedelic pop art in the 1960s. The stretched effect had a big influence on my own artistic endeavours at school from then on, and it soon became *de rigueur* not to be able to easily make out what similar graphics were actually stating on album covers or posters.

However, come the New Year, no one had any inkling that 1966 would prove to be The Beatles' last as a touring group. In hindsight, I only wish I'd been able to see their return to Hammersmith Odeon for one night only on December 10, or their final British concert appearance at the *New Musical Express Poll-Winners Concert*, held at Wembley's Empire Pool on May 1, 1966. They topped an incredible bill which included the Rolling Stones, The Who, The Yardbirds, Roy Orbison, Cliff Richard and the Shadows, Small Faces, Dusty Springfield, The Walker Brothers, and Dave Dee, Dozy, Beaky, Mick & Tich.

I vaguely remember being aware of the show at the time, but have no idea why I didn't try to get a ticket or ask the folks to help out, as Wembley Park was just a few tube stops from Stanmore. Then, 10 years later, I became friendly with a record label colleague, Adam Kinn, whose father Maurice founded the *New Musical Express,* and who also promoted the concert. Adam not only went to the show as a youngster, but also met The Beatles backstage, got their autographs and even sat on Lennon's lap. Lucky lad.

*

As the summer of 1966 kicked in, millions of people around the country were looking forward to the World Cup football finals, to be held in England that summer, while the pop charts were exploding with songs by many acts from that *NME* show among others. I was enjoying it all, mainly via *Top of the Pops, Ready Steady Go!, Thank Your Lucky Stars* and also the pop press, especially the weeklies: *New Musical Express, Record Mirror, Disc & Music Echo,* and *Melody Maker.*

Years later I got to know some of the journalists on those papers extremely well, such as Keith Altham, Nigel Hunter, Chris Welch and Chris Charlesworth. We're all good pals today but, at the time, they were just names on a page whose articles I keenly read without knowing anything about the people behind them.

Then there was *Fabulous* and the monthly *Rave* magazine, which despite containing articles appealing more to girls than boys, always had great pop features and photos. Plus, of course, the monthly *Beatles Book* magazine, which I bought religiously as soon as each issue came out. This was the most essential read for Fab Four fans, covering all the latest news along with juicy tid-bits of information about what the boys were up to in the studio, on tour or just relaxing at home.

Looking back, it does seem slightly strange that I was reading it each month pretty much in isolation, not knowing any other die-hard Beatles fans in our area to discuss them with. Nigel liked them too but was developing more of an interest for vintage rock'n'roll, with Bill Haley & His Comets among his early record purchases.

Inevitably, many of the articles and photos in those journals and others ended up in my Beatles scrapbooks, my own personal record of the Swinging '60s, with a mop-top bias. I was also a paid-up member of the official Beatles Fan Club, which as well as sending out regular newsletters also despatched the legendary Beatles Christmas records, issued on flexi-discs, which I eagerly looked forward to receiving each year.

The group recorded these special discs from 1963 up to 1969, distributing them free of charge in colourful printed sleeves to all fan club members. Receiving these extremely entertaining — and often hilarious — records in the mail each

December was a real highlight of the festive season: without a doubt, The Beatles were the group that never stopped giving.

Nigel and I especially enjoyed the 1966 disc, *Pantomime: Everywhere It's Christmas* and 1967's *Christmas Time Is Here Again,* both featuring surrealist audio sketches and catchy seasonal songs. If you ever hear anyone quietly whispering, 'Matches, candles … matches, candles' or shouting, 'Operator, operator', then you'll know exactly what I'm talking about.

*

At the time I had a good pal at school named David Templer, who happened to live in St. John's Wood, just a short distance from EMI Studios in Abbey Road. He often told me that he'd seen The Beatles arriving at the studios during the holidays and at other times, not so surprising as it was a mere two-minute walk for him. He even managed to get his copy of the *Help!* album signed by the group, which soon got me thinking that I should really try and get some of this real-life Beatles action for myself. So, during the Easter holidays of 1966, I cycled to David's family flat on Grove End Road, the continuation of Abbey Road going towards the West End.

David had been given a drum kit for his 13th birthday and bar mitzvah, which he kept in his bedroom but mistakenly had set it up back to front, with the bass drum on the left and hi-hat stand to the right. As soon as I saw him playing, rather well I thought, I was desperate to have a go on the kit myself. My life-long love of drums and drumming began that very morning, as I bashed along — left-handed, still to this day thanks to David's error — to 'Nowhere Man', The Who's 'Substitute' and the Small Faces' 'Sha La La La Lee', as spun on his handy Dansette record player.

I was instantly hooked, and vowed to get myself a kit as soon as possible, building one up piece-by-piece quite soon afterwards with Dad's help as driver. The main point of this story being, that I started playing the drums for the very first time on the same day that my favourite Beatle jokingly swore at me, just an hour or two later.

David suggested we should head down to EMI Studios to see if there was anything going on, so we stopped messing around on the drum kit and had some lunch made by his Mum. For some reason, I walked my bicycle the short distance to the studios, where we encountered a group of fans — mainly female — waiting for something to happen. Quite normal procedure, I was assured by David, so I placed my bike against one of the studio gates (the one on the far left looking from the road) and we joined the waiting crowd.

A short while later, we spotted a huge black Rolls Royce Phantom V slowly approach the studios. However, not only could we see it, but could also hear its famous occupant, thanks to a loudspeaker hidden inside the wheel arches and wired up to a microphone inside. An extremely familiar voice with a Liverpool accent was speaking complete nonsense as the Rolls neared us, surprising us all with a hilarious Goons-like spoof commentary, of which the only words I can remember as the car made its final approach were,

"And get that bloody bike out of the way!"

Indeed, it was none other than John Winston Lennon, MBE. All in a fluster I hurriedly moved my cycle away from the studio gate in order to allow the huge vehicle to enter the car park, followed by all the excited fans, who quickly surrounded it. A few seconds later, John — wearing trendy tinted sunglasses — jumped out and rushed up the steps to vanish through the hallowed entrance, and that was suddenly it.

I was so surprised by what had happened that it took a few moments to sink in: I'd been given a direct instruction by the chief Beatle, which I had to act on pretty damn quickly. David and I both laughed at the madness of it all, hanging around the studio entrance for a while longer, but no one else turned up during that time. I eventually said my goodbyes to him, with the full intention of returning on another occasion, which I did a week or so later, this time armed with my trusty Kodak Brownie camera.

Sadly, no Beatles arrived on that occasion, or maybe they were already inside the building or turned up later, but I did manage to snap producer George Martin walking up the steps (blink and you'll miss him) as well as Frank Ifield on the street, plus Graham Nash of The Hollies arriving by car. It later became apparent that The Beatles had been working on 'Paperback Writer' or 'Rain' on or around the day that I encountered John Lennon in person for the first time, or rather on the day when he first encountered me.

Frank Ifield outside EMI Studios, 1966

CHAPTER 3

I'D LOVE TO TURN YOU ON

'Paperback Writer' was released on May 30, 1966, and became an instant smash hit thanks to its catchy opening guitar riff, great tune and extremely clever lyrics, mainly written by Paul, in the form of a letter from an unemployed writer to a book publisher. As John later said, it was really, 'the son of 'Day Tripper'', but it became one of my favourite Beatles songs, not least as it seemed to catch the mood of mid-'60s pop art literary culture so well. Meanwhile on the flip-side, Lennon's brilliant 'Rain' is still considered by many drummers as one of the finest examples of Ringo's playing, his inventive fills colouring a seminal song, which seemed to be marking some interesting changes to come in The Beatles' ongoing musical progression.

This soon became fully apparent on August 5 with the release of the *Revolver* album, along with another double A-side single, 'Eleanor Rigby'/'Yellow Submarine', released on the same day. The album was full of other terrific songs, from John's 'I'm Only Sleeping' and 'She Said, She Said' to Paul's 'Got To Get You Into My Life' and 'For No One', plus George's 'Taxman' and 'I Want To Tell You'. But it was the final track on the record which mostly grabbed my attention at the time, John's weird and hypnotic 'Tomorrow Never Knows'. I became fascinated by this mystical masterpiece and remember thinking that, like 'Rain', it must surely represent the future direction of pop music, being so unlike anything that The Beatles or anyone else had to offer.

The group seemed to be leading the western world's young generation into uncharted waters with this track, which I thought was deliberately placed at the end of the album as a trailer of things to come. In other events, the England football team won the World Cup just six days before *Revolver* was released, the entire country enjoying a short period of relative euphoria. At the same time, the Vietnam War was escalating in south-east Asia as The Beatles toured the United States from August 12, culminating on August 29 at Candlestick Park in San Francisco, where ticket prices ranged in price from $3.80 to an exorbitant $7.

However, within a couple of months we knew that last end-of-tour show was actually The Beatles' final paid-performance, as the group had decided to pack up touring for good. They were soon to start work on a new album, which the *Beatles Book* monthly had already hinted as being something very special indeed. Then, in October, the Beach Boys released 'Good Vibrations', a record so perfectly beautiful and original that it caught pretty much everyone by surprise. Incredible harmonies, weird instrumentation, and hard-to-fathom lyrics: this extremely progressive creation by America's only real challengers to The Beatles was a real game-changer, and won The Beach Boys an *NME* award the following year as 'World's Top Vocal Group'.

We didn't quite know it then, but by the end of 1966 the fight was on, with The Beatles working flat-out on what was to be later hailed as pop music's greatest achievement, *Sgt. Pepper's Lonely Hearts Club Band*, although still six months away from release. But first the magnificent double A-side single, 'Penny Lane'/'Strawberry Fields Forever' was issued in February 1967, the latter song confirming my suspicions about the group's — or at least John's — future musical direction, with its highly unusual sounds, obscure lyrics and weird structure.

By contrast, Paul's 'Penny Lane' was a wonderfully melodic and lyrically astute reflection on his Liverpool roots, and most likely would have been a surefire No. 1 if the record hadn't been issued as a double A-side. Instead of which, it was famously held off the top spot by Engelbert Humperdinck's 'Release Me', which annoyed me intensely at the time. The Beatles' majestic new single arrived in a picture-sleeve portraying the four former mop-tops as extremely grown-up young men with newly-grown moustaches, along with images of them as babies or youngsters on the reverse. The times they were certainly a-changing.

*

The start of 1967 also saw an unlikely newcomer, from Seattle on America's west coast, suddenly make a huge impact on British music fans. In January, the Jimi Hendrix Experience exploded on to the UK charts with 'Hey Joe', supported by the group's appearances on television and in the music press. I was immediately smitten by Jimi's incredible look and sound, as were many of my school-pals. The band's early television spots on *Ready Steady Go!* and *Top of the Pops* were easily the main subject of playground conversation the following day.

No one had ever seen or heard anyone like Hendrix before, so when I spotted a small advertisement in the London *Evening Standard* for the band's first major London appearance, I immediately booked tickets for no less than six of us school chums. Hendrix was booked to support The Who on January 29 at the Saville Theatre, which was leased every Sunday by Brian Epstein and NEMS. Booking the tickets was quite an achievement in itself, as I'd never been to a pop concert with anyone other than family before. This was to be my first major rock show with friends.

Off I went that Sunday evening to Shaftesbury Avenue, located off Cambridge Circus, to meet the lads at the Saville Theatre, now the Odeon Cinema. The building still retains its iconic sculptured frieze above the entrance, representing 'Drama Through the Ages', as designed by Gilbert Bayes in 1930. I'm pretty sure we must have been the youngest members of the audience at just 13 and 14 years old.

The show was an amazing experience (to coin a phrase), especially for a bunch of schoolboys to witness, and one which was also destined to enter rock's history books. I was totally captivated by Jimi Hendrix, a mesmerising performer who had excellent support from bassist Noel Redding and drummer Mitch Mitchell. While Ringo and Keith Moon were my drum idols, it was obvious that Mitch was another huge talent who was to have a profound effect and influence on my playing. I would soon be trying to emulate him at home, playing along with Experience tracks on my Broadway drum kit, as set up in the spare room where I had also installed a primitive amp, speaker and turntable.

The band's set included 'Hey Joe', 'Like A Rolling Stone' and, most memorably, Hendrix's stunning version of 'Wild Thing': we'd certainly never heard anything like this before. Jimi was an instant hit who was about to change all the rules with his sensational playing, wild man image and incendiary stagecraft. The key to it all was his superb songwriting and interpretation, along with the band's unique ability to transform his adventurous tunes into rock classics, with a distinctly jazz-tinged rhythm edge, thanks to Mitch's extremely classy playing.

Next up were The Who, the band I was destined to see many times over the next 50 years, but this was my first chance of witnessing this musical power-house, whose early records I loved. They certainly didn't disappoint, shaking the Saville with a dynamic explosion of volume and energy. I was completely entranced by Keith's maniacal drumming and facial expressions; Pete's 'windmill' guitar antics, on-stage chat and jokes; John's stoic stance and deft bass-playing; and Roger's glorious soaring vocals.

I had only just bought their second album, *A Quick One,* featuring Alan Aldridge's superb pop art cover, from which they performed 'A Quick One While He's Away', or the 'mini-opera' as it was more commonly known. The Who were just astounding: four distinct personalities all gelling as one. This was despite often succumbing to on-stage arguments, which we loved to encourage, while (almost) always delivering the most inspirational and unforgettable performances. For the next few years at least, this was live rock music at its highest level.

The evening was made doubly historic, as all four Beatles turned up for the second show and were seated in the royal box up in the circle. Although we were halfway back in the stalls and couldn't actually see them, I still treasure the fact that my three (still) favourite acts — The Beatles, The Who, and Hendrix — were all in the same place as I was, for one night only. I went on to see The Who and Hendrix playing separately at the Saville that year and beyond, but January 29,

1967 was the date on which I was inducted into swinging London's palace of rock royalty: it didn't get much better than that.

*

Meanwhile the spring and early summer of 1967 were full of anticipation, as the next Beatles album would eventually be released on June 1st. I heard a preview of *Sgt. Pepper* on Kenny Everett's show on pirate station Radio London, and like many others was originally quite bemused by it: being so different on every level, it took quite a few listens to eventually take in properly. It was only after the songs became more familiar that its musical brilliance, lyrical genius and the wistful humour in many of its outstanding tracks became completely apparent.

The Beatles had surpassed themselves with a quite revolutionary album made up of some of the most iconic songs of the decade, not least the majestic closing track, 'A Day in the Life'. In addition, the brilliant Peter Blake-designed sleeve, with its remarkable front cover; printed lyrics on the reverse; free cut-outs; and patterned inner sleeve also proved beyond any doubt that the group were still very much the Kings of Pop, just five years on from their 1962 debut 'Love Me Do', which now sounded somewhat primitive. The 'Summer of Love' had officially arrived, heralded by *Sgt. Pepper's Lonely Hearts Club Band*, which would occupy the top of the UK charts for a record 27 weeks.

The album's title song was famously covered by Jimi Hendrix at his Saville Theatre show on June 4, just three days after *Sgt. Pepper* was released. I was back there to witness it, along with Paul McCartney and George Harrison, not that I was sitting anywhere them. I'd have to wait another year for that. It was quite extraordinary to hear Jimi turn The Beatles' brand-new track into a Hendrix belter to open the show with, taking everyone present by complete surprise. It's worth reprinting here what Paul thought about it some years later:

"Jimi was a sweetie, a very nice guy. I remember him opening at the Saville on a Sunday night, 4th June 1967. Brian Epstein used to rent it when it was usually dark on the Sunday. Jimi opened, the curtains flew back and he came walking forward, playing 'Sgt. Pepper', and it had only been released on the Thursday so that was like the ultimate compliment. It's still obviously a shining memory for me because I admired him so much anyway, he was so accomplished. To think that that album had meant so much to him as to actually do it by the Sunday night, three days after the release.

"He must have been so into it, because normally it might take a day for rehearsal and then you might wonder whether you'd put it in, but he just opened with it. It's a pretty major compliment in anyone's book. I put that down as one of the great honours of my career. I mean, I'm sure he wouldn't have thought of it as an honour, I'm sure he thought it was the other way round, but to me that was like a great boost." — Paul McCartney.

Jimi's support acts that night included ex-Moody Blues singer Denny Laine (later to join Paul in Wings); US girl group The Chiffons (whose 1963 single 'He's So Fine' would later cause George so many headaches); and mysteriously-named new outfit Procol Harum. Just two weeks later, they would hit the No. 1 spot with their enigmatic, timeless debut single 'A Whiter Shade Of Pale' on Decca's Deram label, very much the other sound of '67.

During the show's interval, I sneaked into the backstage garden behind the theatre, where Procol Harum were doing a quick photo-shoot for the following week's *Record Mirror*, with singer and pianist Gary Brooker dressed in a striking black and white kimono and Chinese-style hat. I stood there for a few moments, quietly watching the session before heading back into the theatre for Jimi's performance, which also included 'Foxy Lady', 'Like a Rolling Stone', 'Manic Depression', 'Hey Joe', 'Purple Haze', 'The Wind Cries Mary', and finally 'Are You Experienced'.

That closing track was also the title of Jimi's debut album, released three weeks before *Sgt. Pepper,* and one which I'd already played many times. I was fortunate to see him performing live on six occasions in total: three times at the Saville Theatre, twice at the Royal Albert Hall and finally in August 1970 on the Isle of Wight. On the last day of the famous festival, I was unexpectedly given a VIP pass by a female photographer I'd met two weeks earlier in the south of France (long story). I ended up in a wooden seat just 20 feet from the stage for the rest of the day, sitting next to Tony Joe White (of 'Polk Salad Annie' fame), while the rest of my friends were stuck halfway back in an estimated crowd of 600,000. Sorry chaps, but it had to be done.

Jimi may not have given the best performance of his career that night, as he didn't appear until the early hours after being introduced by MC Jeff Dexter. He was as tired as the rest of us and beset by some technical problems during his headline spot, but I didn't care. It was just great to see him at such close quarters, with Billy Cox replacing Noel on bass and Mitch giving it all on drums, classy as ever. Although it was pretty dark, if you look very closely you may be able to see me somewhere near the front.

Three weeks later, on Friday September 18, 1970, Jimi was found dead from an overdose of barbiturates — a huge shock. On the way home from school, I picked up a copy of the *Evening Standard* (which I still have) and was shattered from the moment I saw the unbelievable headline. James Marshall Hendrix was, without doubt, the most electrifying guitarist and one of the most dynamic live performers of all time. Rock on Jimi.

*

Back in 1967, it's still hard to take in that The Beatles were working hard on their next non-album single, just two weeks after *Sgt. Pepper* was released, with initial sessions for 'All You Need Is Love' taking place at Olympic Studios in Barnes. The group's performance of the song was to be the finale and highlight of the BBC's section of the *Our World* global satellite broadcast on June 25. The programme had taken 10 months to put together — involving more than 10,000 personnel around the world — and attracted up to 700 million viewers, a record for its day. Apart from The Beatles' contribution, the two-and-a-half-hour show featured spots by such diverse artists as Maria Callas and Pablo Picasso, while 'All You Need Is Love' was scheduled for single release on Ringo's birthday, July 7.

I watched the programme at home with Nigel, Mum and Dad on our brand-new colour television set, as BBC2 had just begun broadcasting in that format on July 1. However, *Our World* was annoyingly shown on BBC1 in black and white, with just 14 countries participating instead of the originally planned 18, as the USSR and three other Eastern Bloc countries pulled out four days earlier in protest at the Six-Day War in the Middle East.

Like millions of others, we waited patiently through all the various international performances, of which I remember precisely zilch, before the BBC cameras at EMI Studios in Abbey Road were finally turned on at 9.54pm for the British section. Which of course started promptly with the French national anthem, 'La Marseillaise', played as the surprising introduction to The Beatles' new song. And there the group suddenly was, looking suitably psychedelic in their (presumably) colourful clothing while accompanied by a full orchestra, although The Beatles were actually playing to a pre-recorded backing track.

John had written 'All You Need Is Love' very much as a slogan for the 'Summer of Love', using simplistic words in the chorus quite deliberately so that people of every nationality could easily understand it. The verse lines were slightly more obscure, but it didn't matter: the music was the message, and the word was love. It was also exciting to see various Beatle buddies among the studio audience, including Mick Jagger, Marianne Faithfull, Keith Richards, Keith Moon, Eric Clapton, Graham Nash, Mike McGear, Tony Bramwell, Pattie Boyd, and Jane Asher.

Our small family audience all enjoyed The Beatles' historic performance, as Brian Epstein must surely also have done, especially as he looked so proud of the group in photos taken during rehearsals. However, 'All You Need Is Love' would sadly prove to be the very last record released by his world-conquering clients during his lifetime.

CHAPTER 4

BABY YOU'RE A RICH MAN

In late August 1967 I was on holiday with the family in Majorca, staying at Hotel Victoria in Palma, built rather like a luxurious fortress but considered the best hotel on the island. By coincidence, one year later Jimi Hendrix also visited Palma to play at a new discotheque named Sgt. Pepper's, co-owned by his managers, Chas Chandler and Mike Jeffrey. Anyway, I was strolling through the hotel foyer at around lunchtime on Monday, August 28 - a Bank Holiday back home - when I happened to spot a rather familiar looking female checking in at reception.

It was pop singer Sandie Shaw, of barefoot performing fame, who just three months earlier won the Eurovision Song Contest for the United Kingdom with 'Puppet On A String' written by Bill Martin and Phil Coulter. A year later, Bill bought John Lennon's house, 'Kenwood', in Weybridge from him and eventually became a friend of mine. Sadly, he died in March 2020. Another good songwriter pal of ours, Barry Mason, coincidentally bought George Harrison's house, 'Kinfauns', in Esher in 1970.

I could hear Sandie talking to a couple of people at reception about a terrible tragedy which had occurred the day before: Brian Epstein had apparently been found dead at his London home in Chapel Street, Belgravia, due to unknown causes. Naturally, I was incredibly shocked to hear this unthinkable news. By the time the English newspapers arrived in Palma early that afternoon, it was already the main subject of pool-side conversation, thanks to Sandie's sad but timely information.

It was hard to believe that 'Eppy' was dead: as we had no idea whatsoever what had caused it at the time, we could only assume it was either by taking his own life or an accidental overdose. I was most upset, especially after having met his brother Clive just three years earlier, also while on holiday. By coincidence, one of the tracks I vividly remember being played in the local Spanish bars and cafés during the holiday was 'Baby You're A Rich Man', the B-side of 'All You Need Is Love' and also a Lennon song, later said to have been written with Brian in mind.

At the end of the week we arrived back home, where I gathered a pile of press cuttings to create a special tribute to Brian in one of my three Beatles scrapbooks for 1967. It also included photos and quotes by The Beatles, who learned the shocking news during their trip to Bangor in Wales, where they had travelled to study with the Maharishi Mahesh Yogi. It all seemed so ironic and just a little morbid that they should be comforted by their newly-adopted Indian guru and mentor while their long-time manager, friend, and 'fifth Beatle', Brian, lay dead in a London morgue. Especially as they were now exploring spiritual pastures new in that heady summer of peace, love and optimism.

*

By coincidence, I had been looking forward to seeing, and hopefully meeting, Brian during a planned talk he was due to give to youngsters in September at East Finchley Jewish Youth Club in north London. Epstein was closely involved with the club since becoming vice-president in 1964. His main duty there was to present the 'Brian Epstein Awards' for drama and public speaking each year, as well as dropping into the premises occasionally for a visit. I sometimes went to the club for its Sunday night discos, so kept my eyes and ears open for any information and updates about what would happen now that Brian was dead.

In fact, it was announced quite quickly that his visit would be honoured by his mother, Malka 'Queenie' Epstein, who would visit the club on the date originally arranged for her late son. Naturally I went along, to witness a rather frail-looking Queenie breaking down in tears most of the time, surrounded by a crowd of deeply sympathetic kids, plus some parents and others. Younger son Clive was there with her too, a traumatic occasion for both. To compound their grief, his father, and Queenie's husband, Harry Epstein, died just one month before Brian, so it was a wretched time for both of them. I remember Queenie talking briefly about Brian and saying a few words of thanks to us all, but she was crying so much that it was hard to make out a lot of what she was saying.

She and Clive left the room fairly quickly, to be consoled and thanked by club officials, while I managed to offer a few brief words of condolence to them both.

A month later, on Wednesday, October 18, my pal David Templer hinted at school that he was going somewhere 'rather special' that evening, but had been sworn to secrecy about it. Of course, I was highly curious to learn what it was all about, but I didn't find out until later that night when I watched the news on TV. All four members of The Beatles had attended a memorial service for Brian Epstein at the New London Synagogue, just a few blocks down from EMI Studios on Abbey Road.

I couldn't believe it, especially as I knew the son of Rabbi Dr. Louis Jacobs, who officiated at the service: David Jacobs was Templer's best pal and also lived in St. John's Wood. I'd become friendly with him as well over the previous year, and he's still one of my closest friends. To be fair, David (Jacobs) apologised profusely after the event, saying that his father told him that he could only invite one person, and that they were lucky to be there at all. I was both pleased for them and at the same time pretty envious: who wouldn't want to be in the same place as The Beatles, whatever the circumstances. Little did I know then that such an opportunity would present itself to me less than a year later, and on a much more joyous occasion.

*

The rest of 1967 was dominated by many memorable album releases, including *The Who Sell Out*, Hendrix's *Axis Bold As Love*, Cream's *Disraeli Gears, The Doors*, and the Bonzo Dog Doo-Dah Band's *Gorilla*, among others. However, it was The Beatles' *Magical Mystery Tour* double EP and television film which I was most looking forward to.

The film had been much talked about in the press, as filming had started just two weeks after Epstein's death, with The Beatles (especially Paul) having motivated themselves to continue working after the tragedy. The EP set was released on December 8, in the same week that 'Hello Goodbye', backed by 'I Am the Walrus', reached No. 1, thereby keeping the *Magical Mystery Tour* EP off the top spot.

It was a positively Beatles-dominated Christmas, with the film itself screened by BBC1 on Boxing Day in black and white. Like the majority of viewers, I was slightly confused by it all, apart from loving the already-familiar songs. Nevertheless, I enjoyed the often-surrealist coach and comedy sequences, which to me seemed rather like a visual version of the Christmas fan-club records.

It all made better sense when it was repeated by BBC2 on January 5, 1968, but this time shown in colour. That made a huge difference. As usual, The Beatles were ahead of their time: within a couple of years, 'Monty Python's Flying Circus' would make a huge impact with much the same kind of silly humour and random jokes without endings. By coincidence, four of the future Pythons — Eric Idle, Terry Jones, Michael Palin, and Terry Gilliam — featured in new ITV children's series, *Do Not Adjust Your Set*, which began its run on December 26, just a few hours before *Magical Mystery Tour* was initially screened.

The other act common to both that series and The Beatles' TV film was the afore-mentioned Bonzo Dog Doo-Dah Band. I was already very familiar with the *Gorilla* album, released in October, which Nigel and I loved and played a lot, especially enjoying 'The Intro and The Outro' and 'Jollity Farm'. The Bonzos were the most anarchic British musical comedy act of all time, quite hilarious on records, stage and television. I saw them live on a few occasions, the first time being in April 1968, when they supported The Who at the Marquee Club's 10th anniversary celebrations, as Jethro Tull did the following night. The Bonzos actually stank the place out by stringing a few cuts of rotting meat along the top of the stage, which even Keith Moon complained about when The Who came on. But it was all extremely funny.

For their spot in *Magical Mystery Tour,* the Bonzos performed 'Death Cab For Cutie', written by Neil Innes and Vivian Stanshall, and filmed at Raymond's Revue Bar in Soho, one of London's most famous strip clubs. (The previous year we'd met Paul Raymond and his family on holiday, and I stayed friends with his son Howard for a short while). In the sequence, The Beatles and other male coach passengers are seen sitting in the club, all ogling an attractive and voluptuous stripper played by Jan Carson, who interacts with the Bonzos as she discards all her clothes, along with an extremely revealing pink feather boa. This hot-blooded 15-year old was quite turned on by that scene at the time, while the uncensored version currently available on YouTube is even racier.

Many years later, the great Vivian Stanshall became a subscriber to my *SongLink* magazine for a while, not long before he tragically died in a fire at his top-floor flat in Muswell Hill, north London in March 1995. One of the great eccentrics of British music and comedy, Vivian is still revered for his hilarious performances, lyrics and recordings, along with his unique broadcasts on BBC Radio One, produced by John Walters.

The other Beatles connection with the Bonzos is that Paul McCartney produced their classic 1968 single, 'I'm the Urban Spaceman' with Gus Dudgeon (another much-missed pal), under the pseudonym Apollo C. Vermouth. The song was written and sung by Neil Innes, whom I got to know through his involvement with BASCA, also sharing jury duty with him and others at the Cavan Song Contest in Ireland.

A decade after *Magical Mystery Tour,* Neil acted as lead singer and songwriter for The Rutles' brilliant TV spoof *All You Need Is Cash,* the cast also including Eric Idle, Ricky Fataar and John Halsey, with cameo appearances by George Harrison, Mick Jagger and Paul Simon. Neil also worked extensively with the Monty Python team and in bands such as Fatso and Grimms, as well as releasing many solo records. Sadly, he died after a sudden heart attack in December 2019, so farewell (once again) to the great Ron Nasty, forever 'Number One, Number One'.

CHAPTER 5

WE ALL LIVE IN A YELLOW SUBMARINE

I t was in 1968 that I experienced my most memorable Beatles encounter. The previous few months saw *Sgt. Pepper* dominate the album charts, followed by the *Magical Mystery Tour* (EP) and 'Hello Goodbye' singles, which remained in the UK Top 10 until the end of January. I was still at school but continued to follow events with as much interest as ever. 'Hello Goodbye' was succeeded at the top spot in March by Paul's clever piano boogie, 'Lady Madonna', coupled with George's mystical 'The Inner Light' — a highly appropriate song to release during the group's trip to Rishikesh that winter to meditate with the Maharishi Mahesh Yogi.

It was fascinating to read the daily press reports about The Beatles' activities in India, along with celebrity friends like Donovan, Mike Love of the Beach Boys, Mia Farrow, and others. Less than two weeks later, Ringo and Maureen returned home early, mainly because the food didn't agree with Ringo's sensitive stomach — despite taking a case-full of Heinz baked beans with him. Paul returned in late March, followed by John and George in mid-April, before the group continued work on the new songs they'd written at the ashram before starting sessions for their next album in May.

The summer's big Beatles event was the planned release of the animated feature film, *Yellow Submarine,* for which pre-publicity was already in motion by late spring. The date of July 17 was set for the world premiere at the London Pavilion in Piccadilly Circus, the same cinema at which both *A Hard Day's Night* and *Help!* had originally been screened. The third Beatles movie premiere in the West End would prove to be an extremely newsworthy occasion, as relatively few people in the country had seen the group all together in public since their final performance at Wembley's Empire Pool back in May 1966.

Two years on, The Beatles' looks and personal situations were, in most cases, markedly different. John had recently replaced wife Cynthia with little-known Japanese artist Yoko Ono, who would be accompanying him to a major Beatles event for the first time. Paul had just broken off his engagement with actress Jane Asher, his girlfriend for almost five years, and who, like Cynthia, had also been with the group in India. George was, for a few years yet, still with Pattie, as well as being the main influence behind the trip to Rishikesh, and had also recorded *Wonderwall Music*, the first solo album to be released by any Beatle. And Ringo? He'd been pre-occupied with his part-owned construction company, Bricky Builders, and doing up his house in Weybridge, as well as bringing up young sons Zak and Jason with Maureen.

The Beatles had gone psychedelic during 1967 and all Indian-mystic in early 1968, so what would they do next? Ah yes, of course – a cartoon film for kids of all ages, based on their most child-like and infuriating hit song. Why ever not?

So it was that, at around 3 o'clock in the afternoon of Wednesday, July 17th, I arrived at Piccadilly Circus with yet another pal named David (naturally). This time it was David Harris, who wasn't especially a huge Fabs fan like myself, but quite happy to come along for the fun of it. By the time we arrived, a sizeable crowd had already begun to gather, while security barriers were just being put in place outside the cinema.

The entire frontage of the Pavilion boasted an enormous display announcing *The Beatles Yellow Submarine,* along with huge cut-outs of their cartoon characters. The excitement was beginning to mount even though the big event was still a few hours away. Suddenly, as I was surveying the scene from our vantage point by the statue of Eros, I spotted somebody entering an unassuming door, located right next to the cinema's main entrance. I quickly said to David,

"Let's go and see where that leads..."

So off we headed to the door in question, which quite remarkably was unlocked. A few seconds later we were inside, and immediately found ourselves looking at another door, but this time it was the entrance to a lift. We entered it, pressed the highest button and headed up to the top floor, where we found a small flight of steps leading up to the roof. We climbed up and gingerly stepped out, not having the slightest clue as to who or what we might find up there.

What we didn't expect to find was a gathering of other fans, at least a dozen or more, and mainly French for some reason. They obviously had the same idea as us and found their way up there. They were mostly a bit older than us, with some of them smoking (I knew not what), drinking and treating their somewhat illegal presence there as an excuse for a bit of a party.

The view from the rooftop was quite spectacular: we could see huge numbers of people gathering below, which eventually became a crowd estimated at 60,000 or more, all waiting for The Beatles and their guests to arrive. And there we were, looking down on them and taking it all in, chatting to the Frenchies and wondering what the hell we were going to do next.

Eventually, at around seven o'clock, limousines and taxis began to arrive and started dropping off the guests, although it was quite impossible to make out who they were from our lofty position. I said to David that we should try and get into the cinema and see if we could somehow find a couple of seats, or at least soak in some of the atmosphere before inevitably being chucked out by someone in authority.

On reflection, I must have had an inkling that I was going to try something that evening, as I was quite smartly dressed in a dark blue Regency-style 'Lord John of Carnaby Street' suit, plus a long-collared turquoise shirt and colourful kipper tie. David was more modestly attired in a blazer, but we both looked the part of smart young lads invited to the event. Which was extremely lucky, as no sooner had we walked back down the steps and into the cinema's upper circle, we were immediately accosted by an usherette who asked to see our tickets.

"Er, sorry, but we handed them in downstairs," I hastily explained.

"Oh, you shouldn't have done that, you need to keep your tickets with you at all times," she replied. "I'll have to get the manager over to try and sort this out."

A few moments later the manager arrived, a shortish chap who was friendly enough but obviously rather suspicious about our non-ticketed presence there. He asked who invited us, so I said the first thing that came into my head.

"We were invited by Clive Epstein, Brian's brother, who I'm sure can vouch for us if we can find him here." Gulp! This was more than a long shot, as it surely meant eviction if we found him and the same if we didn't.

"OK then," replied Mr. Manager, "let's go and look for him."

He led us one floor down to the dress circle, where all the stars and VIP's were gathered, and then through the crowd towards the main bar. As we walked past some well-known guests, I recognised some members of Status Quo, recently in the charts with their first hit single, 'Pictures of Matchstick Men'. But no sign at all of Clive Epstein, which of course I was secretly quite relieved about, as it would have been somewhat embarrassing to say the least if we had actually run into him.

However, as we continued walking, I suddenly spotted a familiar-looking middle-aged man with a bald head and heavy-rimmed glasses. I immediately recognised him as Dick James, The Beatles' music publisher and co-director of Northern Songs. I'd never met him before, but knowing exactly who he was from photographs, I approached him cheerfully, as if I'd known him for ages.

"Hello Dick, we're just looking for Clive Epstein, have you seen him here by any chance?", I asked him quite confidently, to which he replied,

"No, I'm very sorry but he rang me this afternoon to say he was stuck in Liverpool on business and can't make it here tonight after all, such a shame."

On hearing this, Mr. Manager immediately turned to me to say,

"Okay, I can see you know people here, so that's fine, enjoy the film," before hurriedly leaving us.

Bingo! I thanked Dick for this priceless piece of information, and we moved off quickly. So, we were in and safe with management approval, but of course still didn't actually have any seats. However, the most inconspicuous place to stand was at the rear of the dress circle, where a few other stragglers had already gathered.

We'd only been standing there a few minutes, before a sudden barrage of flashlights and noise erupted as John, Yoko and Paul walked in, followed by the constantly-clicking paparazzi and film crews. They all rushed straight down to the front row, with the light in that area quickly turning extremely hazy as a result of all the flashbulbs popping off non-stop.

A few moments later, Ringo and Maureen walked in to join John and Paul down at the front, while last to arrive were George and Pattie, who strode right past us — slightly embarrassing for me, as in an old news-clip of that precise moment I have a totally idiotic expression on my face. George looked quite superb dressed in a bright yellow/orange suit with a matching floppy hat, complete with a *Yellow Submarine* badge. Meanwhile, Pattie was looking like an exotic 1920s film star, clothed beautifully for the occasion, with her hair perfectly styled in ringlets. They quickly walked down the aisle to join the rest of the group, while the paparazzi continued their mission for some final shots of the four Beatles before the film began.

However, as the photographers eventually started walking back up towards us, I suddenly spotted two empty seats in the second row. They were just about visible from our fortuitous vantage point at the back of the dress circle, situated on the aisle directly behind Paul and his guest. We quickly walked down, to discover that the third seat along was occupied by Keith Richards of the Rolling Stones, his blonde German-Italian actress and model girlfriend Anita Pallenberg sitting to his right.

I politely asked Keith whether anyone was due to be occupying the two empty seats on his left.

"Nah, they were meant for Mick and Marianne, but they're away in New York, so you're okay there."

Very obliging of him indeed. So, we sat down to watch the film, courtesy of the absent Mick Jagger and Marianne Faithfull, with eternal thanks and three hail Marys to them both. Keith was on my immediate right; Paul directly in front of me, with John to his right, along with Yoko, Maureen, Ringo, George and Pattie, plus Neil Aspinall. It later transpired that Paul's guest was Pattie's younger sister, Jenny Boyd, who also travelled to Rishikesh, and whom I'd get to meet properly years later.

*

Our situation seemed completely too good to be true: I was half-expecting us to be turfed out of our seats at any time, but all was fine once the lights went down. Fortunately, the programme began with a *Pink Panther* short, which gave us time to get our bearings, and to realise how amazingly lucky we had been to get this far. At the same time, once we were seated, I rather took it for granted that this was where we were meant to be, so did my best to act as cool as possible. As you rather need to do when sitting next to Keef and right behind Lennon and McCartney.

However, it was extremely hard to take my eyes off John, who was sitting directly in my sight-line to the right. He had always been my favourite Beatle, the one I often sketched doodles of at school, and the one whose humour and outspoken attitude had such a huge influence on me, as it had on so many others. Not to mention being the Beatle who had told me off outside EMI Studios two years earlier.

And there he was, just inches away from me, in his trendy all-white suit, black shirt and an Indian-style Talisman necklace around his neck, which he'd been wearing on and off for the past 18 months (years later bought by Noel Gallagher at auction and given to brother Liam).

Despite my confident outward appearance, I was actually quaking inside with nerves for the few minutes before the film began. My thoughts were most definitely that 'It's All Too Much', as the title of George's cosmic new acid-influenced song would shortly proclaim in the film soundtrack. But for now, I was just thrilled to be part of The Beatles' privileged inner circle, if only for the duration of the premiere.

Suddenly, the big moment came, the lights were dimmed and all eyes were glued to the screen for the first public screening of *Yellow Submarine*. And what a fabulous visual and aural experience it proved to be: dazzlingly colourful, witty, brilliantly animated and rich, with Beatles songs both old and new. In other words, a most delightful and magical musical tour for kids of all ages, from eight to 80.

I was quite blown away by it all, particularly the clever early 'Eleanor Rigby' sequence featuring the rooftops, people and streets of Liverpool, along with the city's two football teams and other memorable images. I also loved the superb 'Lucy in the Sky' sequence, with its sensational mix of pop art, random brush-strokes and vivid colours. I quickly found myself becoming almost totally absorbed by what was happening on the screen, while at the same time, half-watching John and what I could see of the other Beatles. I was also greatly enjoying the film's four new Fabs' songs as they came up, and at one point leant over to whisper to Paul, I think after 'Hey Bulldog',

"That was a good one," to which he replied with a quick,

"Oh, thanks!"

The film had a fun story, The Beatles all being transported to Pepperland by Old Fred in his titular yellow submarine, through a series of weird aquatic obstacles; encounters with fantastical monsters; and seas of green and holes. Their mission was to free all the residents of Pepperland, including Sgt. Pepper's Lonely Hearts Club Band, from their fate of having been frozen into statues by the army of music-hating, evil Blue Meanies.

Eventually the Chief Blue Meanie, his assistant Max and the Flying Glove, et al were transformed into music and peace-loving lovey-doveys, thanks to The Beatles singing 'All You Need Is Love' before the film drew to a close — but not before a final live-action sequence by the real Beatles, with Ringo finding 'a hole in my pocket' and John informing us that, 'newer and bluer Meanies have been sighted within the vicinity of this theatre'.

The audience rightly gave *Yellow Submarine* a huge standing ovation, lasting several minutes, while for me it just felt incredible to be applauding right behind the four famous faces who had inspired the entire cinematic experience.

As the prolonged applause slowly died down, I realised that we were completely people-locked, as so many people in the front circle area were trying to congratulate The Beatles. I ended up chatting with John and Yoko for a few moments as they stood trapped in their places, and can just about recall George being politely interested in my high opinion of his two new songs and the film. We then followed him straight to the circle lounge area, where he was quickly surrounded by photographers and reporters, with Pattie looking on as I stood next to him.

A mere 20 years later, I spotted a photograph of this encounter in a special *Yellow Submarine* anniversary edition of the re-issued *Beatles Book* monthly, dated June 1988, and thought to myself, hmm — that chap looks a bit like me. Hang on, it is me!

So that was it, but not quite. David and I hung around the cinema's main foyer for as long we possibly could, while The Beatles and all the other VIP's left for the after-show party at the Royal Lancaster Hotel in Bayswater. We would have loved to have joined them there too, but (a) we didn't know exactly where it was; and (b) we both had to get back to our respective homes before the tubes stopped running.

However, we did experience one more opportunity to feel a part of the proceedings as we eventually stepped outside the cinema, to witness all the police holding back thousands of Beatles fans who had waited patiently for hours, and who were now chanting in deafening unison.

"We all live in a Yellow Submarine..." — a quite unforgettable scene, especially for two young schoolboys to experience.

Of course, we realised that without a lot of luck (and chutzpah) we would have ended up standing outside the cinema all evening and doing exactly the same thing, had things not gone our way in such a spectacular fashion. In addition, throughout it all we pretty much kept our cool by not asking anyone for a single autograph or photo on the night, not least because I'd left my camera at home.

*

A couple of postscripts: two days later, I was walking from St. John's Wood tube station, to visit my friend David Templer at his home once again. In my pocket, I'd kept the front page of the previous day's *Evening News*, featuring a photo of Twiggy with manager and boyfriend Justin de Villeneuve entering the London

Pavilion, as they'd announced their engagement on the night of the premiere.

As I walked down Circus Road towards Grove End Road, who should I bump into but Paul McCartney, who had just left his home in Cavendish Avenue. He recognised me immediately from the premiere and was happy to chat briefly, after which I asked him to sign my newspaper cutting. He duly obliged, so I did obtain at least one nicely personalised memento of the *Yellow Submarine* premiere in the end.

Secondly, at that time I'd been occasionally corresponding with a girl in the USA, whom I'd met through the Pen-Pals column of *The Beatles Book*. She was always extremely interested to hear about my life in London, plus of course anything to do with the Fab Four.

A few days after the premiere, I wrote to her once more, relating in detail the full story of my incredible adventure. A week or two later I received a short reply from her by airmail, effectively informing me that, "I don't believe a word of this so won't be writing to you again."

It was obviously all too much for her.

Sgt. Peppers Club in Majorca, 1967

Top left: The family outside Jesmond Way in Stanmore, 1956. Top right: On holiday in Torquay in 1964, I'm second left.

Left: Portrait of my ancestor, English champion boxer Daniel Mendoza by James Gillray, 1788.

Below left: My first Beatles scrapbook, as started in 1963.

Below right: My snap of George Martin entering EMI Studios in Abbey Road, April 1966.

Above: The one and only time I saw the Beatles on stage, January 1965.
Below right: Brian Epstein plus an invitation to his memorial service.

The *Yellow Submarine* premiere, July 17, 1968.

Below: Standing next to George in the circle lobby.

Bottom: The front dress circle, just moments before we took our seats next to Keith Richards, right behind Paul and guest. L-R: Neil Aspinall, Pattie, George, Ringo, Maureen, Yoko, John, Paul and Jenny Boyd.

Above: That's me circled behind Neil Aspinall and John (with Yoko, hidden) as they arrive at Marylebone Magistrates Court, October 19th 1968.

Below: John and Yoko line up with everyone at the *Rolling Stones Rock And Roll Circus* at Intertel Studios, December 10th 1968. Inset: the invitation.

The Beatles BOOK
DEC. No. 65 2/6
100 BEATLES' SHOW TICKETS TO BE WON

Beatles & Co
3 Savile Row London W1
telephone 01-734 8232

16th June, 1969

D. Stark,
6 Jesmond Way,
STANMORE.
Middlesex.

Dear Prizewinner,

As you know, it has proved impossible for us to fulfil
our original promise of sending you a ticket to a
Beatles TV show as your prize for winning the fan club
competition.

We are really very sorry about this, and have spent a
long time thinking of an alternative which would not be
a mere consolation for the original prize. Anyway, at
last we're able to tell you that your new prize - and we
hope you like it - is to be an advance copy of the Beatles
new album, which at the moment we're expecting to release
towards the end of August.

John, Paul, George and Ringo would all like to congratulate
you on winning, and hope you will accept their apologies
for the delay.

With best wishes.

Yours sincerely,

PETER BROWN.

John Lennon Paul McCartney George Harrison Richard Starkey Apple Corps

The letter I received after winning tickets to the show which never happened.

44

Royal World Premiere

in the presence of
HRH The Princess Margaret,
Countess of Snowdon
in aid of the
National Society for the
Prevention of
Cruelty to Children

Commonwealth United Presents a Grand Film Starring
Peter Sellers & Ringo Starr in "The Magic Christian"
Also starring WILFRID HYDE-WHITE · ISABEL JEANS · CAROLINE BLAKISTON with Guest Stars RICHARD ATTENBOROUGH
LEONARD FREY · LAURENCE HARVEY · CHRISTOPHER LEE · SPIKE MILLIGAN · ROMAN POLANSKI · RAQUEL WELCH
Produced by DENIS O'DELL · Directed by JOSEPH McGRATH · Executive Producers HENRY T. WEINSTEIN & ANTHONY B. UNGER
Screenplay by TERRY SOUTHERN & JOSEPH McGRATH · From the novel by TERRY SOUTHERN · Music by KEN THORNE
Colour by TECHNICOLOR · Released by COMMONWEALTH UNITED ENTERTAINMENT (UK) LTD

At the Odeon Cinema, Kensington for the world premiere of *The Magic Christian*, December 11 1969.

Below: John signed my souvenir programme beneath this portrait of Princess Margaret.

Above left: The London Pavilion, May 20, 1970.

Right: the second letter I received from Peter Brown at Beatles & Co.

Below: My invitation to the *Let It Be* premiere, which none of the Beatles attended as they'd officially broken up by then.

Beatles & Co
3 Savile Row London W1
telephone 01-734 8232

David A. Stark,
6 Desmond Way,
Stanmore,
Middx.

18th February, 1970

Dear David Stark,

Thank you for your letter of the 9th February. I confirm that I have passed to John Lennon the magazine you enclosed.

I regret that I cannot give you any positive information concerning Toronto as there are no confirmed details or dates at this time.

The situation with the "Get Back" premiere - one hopes it will be within the next few months, but again, there are no confirmed dates.

Yours sincerely,

PETER BROWN.

John Lennon Paul McCartney George Harrison Richard Starkey Apple Corps

The Directors of United Artists Corporation Ltd. cordially invite you to attend the Gala Premiere

THE BEATLES

APPLE
An abkco managed company
presents

"Let it be" U

Produced by NEIL ASPINALL Directed by MICHAEL LINDSAY-HOGG
TECHNICOLOR® United Artists

on Wednesday May 20th at 8.00 p.m. for 8.45 p.m.
at the LONDON PAVILION Piccadilly Circus W.1.

DRESS INFORMAL   R.S.V.P. May 13th

Above: the last time I saw John, signing books with Yoko at Selfridges on July 15, 1971. You can just see me at top right of the picture.

Left: with George Harrison and saxophonist Tom Scott, outside Capital Radio, 1974.

Above left: Dick and Stephen James at DJM. Above right: with Marcel Stellman, my former boss at Decca Records.

Right: With Justin Hayward and John Lodge of the Moody Blues at Threshold Records.

CHAPTER 6

HEY JUDE, IT'S YER BLUES

The following month, in August 1968, Nigel and I returned to the Imperial Hotel in Torquay, where we'd met Clive Epstein four years earlier. This time it was without Mum and Dad but with our paternal grandmother Odie, whose husband, our Grandpa Hyman, had died from a heart attack the year before while on holiday in France. Our stay was memorable for a couple of reasons ...

Firstly, because one of our big (or rather small) comedy heroes, Arthur Askey, was also staying at the hotel while starring at the Princess Theatre for the summer season, along with Irish singer Val Doonican, of rocking-chair fame.

We'd previously seen Arthur Askey play Widow Twankey in the *Aladdin* pantomime at the London Palladium five years earlier, along with the show's stars, Cliff Richard and the Shadows. What also delighted us in Torquay, apart from meeting him and getting his autograph, was to see Arthur ask Grandma Odie for a dance to the hotel band during one of his off-show nights. And they were exactly the same height.

Secondly, on a Sunday afternoon, August 18 if I remember correctly, the first-ever broadcast of the new Beatles single 'Hey Jude' was made by Alan Freeman during his *Pick of the Pops* show on BBC Radio One, two weeks ahead of release. Nigel and I were both sitting on our beds in our shared room, eagerly waiting to hear the new record, set to be issued on August 30, the first-ever release on the Beatles' new Apple label.

When it came on, I was completely entranced by Paul's plaintive intro, setting the tone for what would remain my favourite Beatles song for many years, closely matched by 'Strawberry Fields Forever'. I was quite in awe at how melodic it all sounded, and how long it was, at just over seven minutes. This was a ground-breaking and daring departure for the group, while the B-side 'Revolution', also played by Fluff, was by contrast a gritty rocker from John which pretty much captured the political tone of the era.

They were two completely different songs, but then we wouldn't have expected anything less from The Beatles. The only thing that did raise a few eyebrows at the time was the title 'Hey Jude', which like many others of the Jewish faith I initially had slight reservations about. However, these were happily very quickly dispersed, as it became clear that it was just a name used by Paul instead of 'Jules' (aka Julian Lennon), to whom the song was dedicated.

On our return home, I bought the record on the first day of release, as usual. It was exciting to see the Apple logo on the 'Hey Jude' side of the disc, used for the first time, along with the sliced half-apple on the B-side. Not to mention the sleek black slip-sleeve, all very stylish indeed.

It was also exhilarating to see The Beatles' performance of 'Hey Jude' on the *David Frost Show* on September 8, as filmed at Twickenham Studios with a large audience of youngsters, standing all around the group. I only wished I could have been one of them, as that show would eventually prove to be the group's penultimate 'live' performance together.

*

On Friday, October 18, 1968, John and Yoko were busted for drug possession at their flat in Montagu Square, sub-let from Ringo. They were both summoned to appear at Marylebone Magistrates Court the next morning, which I read about in the evening paper the day before. Being a non-school day, I headed up to the courthouse on Marylebone Road to see what was going on. The grandiose building was just a few minutes' walk from Baker Street tube station, and by the time I arrived it had already become mobbed.

I joined the waiting crowd, and it wasn't long before John and Yoko arrived by car, accompanied by Apple boss Neil Aspinall. He kept behind them as they walked towards the building through the huge throng of people. A number of uniformed police officers were attempting to hold the crowd back, but I had a very good view of the couple as they made their way into court for the hearing, which lasted just five minutes. The infamous Sergeant Norman Pilcher, who made his name by nicking pop stars — later serving four years for perjury — duly read the charges against them; Lennon and Ono were both remanded on bail and the case adjourned until November 28.

However, on leaving the court the couple found that their car wasn't ready and waiting for them as they had expected. Amid the scrum of reporters, police and public they huddled closely together, with John doing his best to protect pregnant Yoko before the vehicle arrived. One of the many photographs of this was later used on the rear sleeve of their album, *Unfinished Music No 2: Life With the Lions*, eventually released on May 9, 1969 following Yoko's miscarriage.

When the album came out, I was fascinated by the image of a boy on the right-hand side of the photo, who looked vaguely like me but obviously wasn't. I knew that I had to have been in at least one or two of the shots taken that day, but it wasn't until 1981, when Ray Connolly's biography *John Lennon 1940-1980* was published, that I finally saw one. There I was, pictured standing just behind John, Yoko and Neil Aspinall en route into court.

I was chuffed to see that picture, which has since been used in many other books and articles, and later managed to get hold of a print of it. The drug bust eventually caused huge problems to John when trying to get his Green Card, as required for US residency. By coincidence, the flat at 34 Montagu Square was purchased some years later by a good pal of mine in the music business, Reynold D'Silva of Silva Screen Records, who still owns it today. I've visited it a few times, while an English Heritage blue plaque marking John and Yoko's short tenure there was put up on the building in 2010, of which more later.

*

The next Beatles album, eponymously titled but better known as the double *White Album* was released on November 22, 1968, exactly five years to the day after *With The Beatles*. Again, I bought it on the first day of release and immediately became fully engrossed in it, not just because of the incredible variety of tracks but also by its beautiful packaging; free poster; high-quality colour portrait prints of the group; and the fact that it was the group's first album release on their own Apple label. It just felt great to physically hold and to examine all the contents in detail, which many of my pals also wanted to do when I brought it into school the following Monday to show them.

One of my favourite tracks was John's 'Yer Blues', the grittiest track on the album along with Paul's 'Helter Skelter', but I had no idea that, within a couple of weeks, John would be singing it live on stage at a rather obscure television studio in north-west London, or that I'd be among the audience on that day.

As a regular *New Musical Express* reader, I'd spotted an intriguing item in the weekly paper's news section at the end of November, offering readers, '*First Chance for Stones TV Tickets*' at a special filming session, set to take place in Wembley the following month. I sent off my hand-written application straight away, hoping to get lucky, especially as I'd never seen the Stones before.

A week or so later I received a double-sided card in the post which stated,

"*You are invited to the Rolling Stones' Rock And Roll Circus on Wednesday December 11th, 1968 at the studios of Intertel Television, Wycombe Road, Wembley, Middlesex. Nearest tube: Stonebridge Park (Bakerloo line). Costumes provided.*"

The reverse of the card featured a line drawing of an elephant wearing a blanket, with the event's title inscribed on it in a circus-type font.

On the appointed Wednesday morning I turned up at the studios, again with David Harris, where we joined a queue of other *NME* readers and invited guests. On arrival, we were all given brightly-coloured ponchos and hats to wear over our clothes, which made the entire audience look like a bunch of munchkins.

We sat down on a long bench, three or four rows from the ringside and took in the sights — and smells — of what was surely going to be a momentous day. I only mention smells because there was a highly pungent farmyard odour present throughout the proceedings, thanks to bundles of hay scattered around the studio for the benefit of the horses.

At the business end of the ring, a stage had been constructed with a balcony above it, displaying the *Circus* logo, surrounded by lightbulbs. This was where the Stones would be watching all the other performers from, but first the show had to be introduced in traditional circus style. Mick Jagger was naturally playing the ringmaster, dressed in an appropriate red and white costume, complete with top hat, long black boots and a horse-whip.

The show opened with a full-entourage circus procession led by acrobats in leotards, followed by a Wild West marshall on horseback; his cowgirl; a Red Indian girl, and various dwarves and clowns. All the stars were in costume and holding orchestral instruments, the Stones first up with Mick in the centre brandishing a whip, while Keith and Bill were playing French horns, with Brian Jones on flute and Charlie Watts crashing a pair of cymbals.

John Lennon then followed on trumpet, with Yoko dressed as a witch, Eric Clapton on saxophone, and The Who all playing brass, complete with Keith Moon dressed as a pierrot. Plus, Marianne Faithfull, Jethro Tull, Taj Mahal, and all the other performers: this was obviously going to be a rock'n'roll show unlike any other seen before. But first it had to be opened officially, with Mick reciting these immortal lines:

"You've heard of Oxford Circus, you've heard of Piccadilly Circus, and this is the Rolling Stones' Rock And Roll Circus, and we've got sights and sounds and marvels to delight your eyes and ears - and you'll be able to see the very first one of those in a few moments."

Mick had to retake this two or three times, while everyone waited patiently, before he introduced Jethro Tull as the first act, performing 'A Song For Jeffrey', or rather miming to it. The group featured highly eccentric-looking singer and flautist Ian Anderson, who looked rather like a crazy bearded tramp, and stood on one leg for most of the time. Meanwhile, future Black Sabbath member Tony Iommi was on left-handed guitar as a temporary replacement for Mick Abrahams, who had just left Tull to form his new outfit, Blodwyn Pig.

I'd already seen Jethro Tull twice that year: firstly, back in April when they supported The Who at the Marquee Club's 10th anniversary celebrations; and secondly, when they were the opening act at the first-ever free concert held in Hyde Park on June 29.

Some 30 years later, I co-wrote a short history of all those free concerts — 17 in total from 1968 to 1976 — for the *Masters of Rock* souvenir programme, when non-free concerts resumed in 1996 with The Who, Clapton, Dylan, et al. I wrote it in conjunction with Jeff Dexter, who famously spun the discs at most of those heady, sunny and cannabis-tinged Hyde Park events. We detailed all the artists who played for free over the years, along with some of the stories behind their sets.

So, I was quite pleased to see Jethro Tull for a third time in 1968, but not so delighted to watch them retake their opening spot at least five or six times.

*

At this point, I should mention that (also) in 1995-96, I became involved with the long-awaited video release of the *Rock And Roll Circus* film, which had never been officially seen, apart from The Who's section, which appeared in their 1979 documentary, *The Kids Are Alright*. The story was that the Stones were never happy with their performance and thought that The Who had blown them offstage.

Mick apparently felt he was looking under-par and exhausted from all the day's (and night's) activity, as not only were the Stones unable to play until the early hours of the following morning due to extended set-up delays, but the *Circus* shoot also coincided with his filming duties for Nic Roeg's *Performance*. Meanwhile, Brian Jones was looking noticeably wasted and well out of it by the time the group eventually hit the stage: this was to be his last-ever performance with them. Ironically, it was also my first and only chance to see all the original Stones in the flesh.

The rights to the film, directed by Michael Lindsay-Hogg — who also directed the Beatles' 'Hey Jude' and 'Revolution' clips, plus the *Let It Be* film a month later — were owned by former Stones' manager Allen Klein's ABKCO company, based in New York. As chance would have it, I knew Klein's daughter Robin very well. She was at the time an item with my good pal Mick Gochanaur, a songwriter/producer and engineer I always meet up with when I was in New York.

Robin is an extremely accomplished film editor, and she and Mick acted as producers of the film's restored version, as eventually released in October 1996. But first, they had to try and find all the original footage, which didn't exist in any one location. They flew over to London a few times from 1993-95, slowly piecing it together from old reels found in various states of decay and hidden in obscure places, much of it in Pete Townshend's archive storage unit, as well as in a barn in France, the country the Stones lived in during their early '70s tax exile period.

I was pleased to relate to Robin and Mick my first-hand recollections of being a *Circus* audience member, and to help with identifying who was who on screen, such as Tony Iommi. Later, when I was back in New York on business, we sat down to watch some footage at the old ABKCO offices on Times Square (they've now moved further downtown), which boasted the biggest collection of historic gold discs covering the walls that I've ever seen. Robin surprised me by playing some audience shots in slow motion on a monitor screen, saying,

"Check this out, David I think I found you." And she had. There I was with pal David, sitting in our ponchos and just about visible in a brief shot. Great work, Robin.

The upshot of all this was that I was given a nice credit right at the end of the video, as the last person to be thanked by the Stones, along with 'everybody's Mums'. A few years later, I provided a brief audio commentary for the DVD release, and attended screenings in London with Robin, Mick, Allen Klein, various Universal Music executives, and other media personnel. I remember one of the screenings for a quite unrelated reason, as when I ventured into a Mayfair pub afterwards, I was somewhat surprised to see legendary beat poet Allen Ginsberg sitting there, sipping his pint.

During another visit to New York, I went to see the Stones on their *Bridges to Babylon* tour at Giants Stadium in October 1997. The difference was that I was travelling in a stretch limo with Allen Klein, Robin and Mick, and we naturally had the best seats in the house. Allen wore a Stones tour jacket and generated a typically no-nonsense aura. It might have been a huge occasion for the thousands gathered there for the show, but to Klein it was just business as usual by his former clients, with whom he still maintained a necessary professional relationship, especially with Mick Jagger.

On reflection, it was quite something to have spent some limited time with the man who had not only managed the Stones but also The Beatles. I would have liked to have asked him many questions, but it wasn't the time or place, especially as he was on his mobile phone for most of the trip to the Stones camp and others. However, I did speak to him about the recent case where ABKCO had famously claimed 100 per cent of the writers' share of The Verve's 'Bitter Sweet Symphony'. This was after the group sampled a small section of 'The Last Time' from the Andrew Loog Oldham Orchestra's 1966 album of Stones songs without permission. Allen agreed it was tough luck but that it was purely business, as they should have asked in the first place. Years later, Verve singer Richard Ashcroft announced at the Ivor Novello Awards in 2019 that his songwriting credit had reverted to him by arrangement with Mick, Keith and ABKCO.

That Stones' show at Giants Stadium was quite spectacular, as usual, while the fact that ABKCO still owns the rights to most of the band's '60s song catalogue was highly significant. Especially as the show opened with 'Satisfaction', probably their biggest earner of all from that period.

*

Back to 1968 and I've left the best until last, as I have a rather unique memory of the *Rock And Roll Circus* film shoot still firmly rooted in my mind.

It happened during a break in filming, when I had to answer a call of nature, walking around the circus ring to reach the toilet facilities on the opposite side. As I went through the gap which led to the loos, I was somewhat taken aback to walk past a group of four guys standing together, all facing each other as they held an intimate chat: John Lennon, Mick Jagger, Pete Townshend, and Eric Clapton.

I don't think anyone else saw that unique gathering apart from me. I walked past them, trying to act as cool and disinterested as you do when walking past the biggest rock stars on the planet. The one moment in my 16 years (and since) when I wish I'd had a camera with me, a quite incredible moment, and definitely the icing on the cake for me that day.

One of the day's other highlights was The Who, performing the mini-opera 'A Quick One While He's Away' once again: a superb version for sure, but which to me seemed slightly out of place as it was by then exactly two years old. I would have much preferred to have seen them perform more recent singles like 'Magic Bus' or 'I Can See For Miles', but knowing Pete he probably chose to play what was their longest track quite deliberately. They certainly gave a fantastic performance of it, and as usual I was excited to witness the force of nature known as Keith Moon once more, playing in full manic flow as ever on an eye-catching chrome silver Premier double kit.

We also saw Marianne Faithfull performing 'Something Better', as announced by Charlie Watts, as well as Keith Richards' introduction to fire-eaters Danny Camara and Donate Luna's short spot. However, it was Taj Mahal's version of 'Homer Banks' blues classic, 'Ain't That a Lot Of Love', which almost stole the show for me, being a totally riveting performance of an extremely powerful song, the intro of which was the key influence for 'Gimme Some Lovin'' by the Spencer Davis Group. Taj Mahal's band also featured guitarist Jesse Ed Davis, who later worked extensively with John Lennon, and who possibly met him for the first time on that day.

Frustratingly, David and I eventually had to leave the studio when the audience was switched over for a new bunch of *NME* readers before the final evening session began. A big shame, as we actually missed The Dirty Mac band, with Lennon, Clapton, Keith Richards and Mitch Mitchell performing 'Yer Blues', along with 'Whole Lotta Yoko', featuring a wailing Ms. Ono accompanied by violinist Ivry Gitlis.

We'd also left before the Stones' extremely late night/early morning set, which started with 'Jumping Jack Flash' and included 'Sympathy With The Devil' and 'You Can't Always Get What You Want', before concluding with 'Salt of the Earth'. This number from *Beggar's Banquet* featured just Mick and Keith singing over a backing track while sitting in the audience at the end of the marathon shoot, with some of the crowd (and Pete Townshend) idiot dancing towards the end. Unlucky for us not to be among them, but at least we got to see everyone in the show at extremely close quarters throughout the day, even if not actually performing their sets.

Six months later, I finally got to see the Stones play live, at their free concert in Hyde Park on July 5, 1969, just two days after Brian Jones' untimely death. Sitting quite near the front, I enjoyed their performance, even though it was slightly ragged round the edges. However, their extended version of 'Sympathy for the Devil', along with Rocky Dijon and other African tribal drummers, was an inspired way to close what was a beautiful and totally memorable afternoon.

The music actually continued into the evening, as I also saw The Who again that very same night, supported by Chuck Berry at the Royal Albert Hall for the *Pop Proms,* hosted by Jeff Dexter. We just walked from Hyde Park to the nearby Albert Hall, where the Stones eventually turned up as well, all sitting in a loggia box not far from our seats in the stalls. The next time I saw Mick and Co. was at the Lyceum on the Strand in December, a totally magnificent show featuring tracks from my still-favourite Stones' album, *Let It Bleed.*

*

Meanwhile, The Beatles weren't letting the Stones get it all their own way in the TV specials department. As was quite usual in their friendly rivalry, they often seemed to do things in parallel or take the mickey out of each other — think of the sleeves of *Sgt. Pepper* and *Their Satanic Majesties Request*; or album titles *Let It Be* and *Let It Bleed* for example. So, just as the Stones were about to film the *Rock and Roll Circus* in front of an invited audience, the December 1968 edition of *The Beatles Book* monthly featured a quite extraordinary flash announcement on its front cover:

"100 Beatles' Show Tickets To Be Won."

Inside the magazine was a coupon, entitling '*Fifty lucky readers to receive a pair of tickets*' to what was casually described as '*the world's biggest concert*', based on official information provided by Apple. It seemed that The Beatles were planning to return to live performing by filming their own TV spectacular, reportedly set to take place at London's Roundhouse (actually booked for three nights); an outdoor amphitheatre in Tunisia; or an equally obscure location somewhere around the world.

This was astounding news, so for the second time in a month I immediately responded for the chance of winning tickets to an exclusive show, which would surely go down as one of the most historic events in pop music history. A (hopefully) triumphant return by The Beatles to the concert stage, just two and a half years after exiting San Francisco's Candlestick Park in 1966, would surely even eclipse Elvis Presley's much-touted *Comeback Special '68*, which by coincidence was televised on December 3.

It all seemed too good to be true, and I should have realised that was exactly what it was, if only I'd paid a little more attention to the small print nestling under the ticket offer, which stated:

"At press time it is not possible to tell you the exact dates of the performances, which will be videotaped in colour in the New Year. Neither The Beatles themselves, or their Apple helpers have sorted that out."

But what did I care? I'd sent off my letter with the coupon straight away and eagerly awaited the February edition of *The Beatles Book*, in which the names of all the 50 lucky winners were to be published. Sure enough, my name was included — but sadly by then, the anticipation and excitement of the planned show had been totally dissipated, by the now common knowledge that the entire plan had been abandoned. Things had changed dramatically during the group's extensive sessions at Twickenham Film Studios and at their Apple Studios, resulting in what eventually became the *Let It Be* album and film, which weren't released until May 1970.

While Paul, the eternal showman, was naturally keen on the concert idea, the others weren't as sold on it, George even quitting the band for a few days in early January '69, just as Ringo had the previous August. However, as the eventual film portrays in all its stark rawness, the group finally all agreed to play some of their new material at a one-off lunchtime concert, held on the roof of the Apple building at 3 Savile Row on Thursday, January 30. They were also joined by organist and old friend Billy Preston, an important catalyst in their sudden decision to perform, as he'd been filming with them for the documentary.

Well, thanks very much, chaps for telling me (not): I was at school that day, and only heard about the rooftop show on the news when I got home. What a complete and utter swizz: I'd won tickets for the greatest gig of all time, and what do they do instead? Play a cracking set on their office roof for a few industry pals and girlfriends, along with passers-by below and some office workers, who were enterprising enough to clamber up to nearby roofs or the actual rooftop.

Sadly, there wasn't much I could do about it, other than wait for a promised consolation prize, which *The Beatles Book* monthly announced would be sent in due course.

CHAPTER 7

AS I READ THIS LETTER

It wasn't until four months later that I received a letter typed on 'Beatles & Co' headed paper from 3 Savile Row, dated June 16, 1969, signed by Apple executive Peter Brown and also Ringo Starr, informing me that:

"At last we're able to tell you that your new prize – and we hope you like it – is to be an advance copy of The Beatles' new album, which at the moment we're expecting to release towards the end of August. John, Paul, George and Ringo would like to congratulate you on winning, and hope you will accept their apologies for the delay."

Naturally, I was thrilled to receive the letter, which to me was just as valuable as the promised alternative prize itself, if not more so. How often did schoolboy fans receive an official missive from The Beatles' HQ, and signed by one of them?

Eventually, I received my advance copy of *Abbey Road* about a week earlier than its release date of September 26. It turned up in a standard brown-card mailer, with no special record label or letter enclosed. However, that particular album copy has stayed quite special to me. Apart from still being my favourite Beatles long player, it's been a constant reminder that I could have been present at that aborted TV special, if the group hadn't changed their minds without telling me, the swines.

Somewhat surprisingly, that letter wasn't the only correspondence from a Beatle I received that month. I was about to get one of the surprises of my life thanks to the release of John & Yoko's afore-mentioned *Unfinished Music #2 – Life With the Lions*, the follow-up to *Two Virgins*, released on the Zapple label. The album's first side featured some cat-wailing by Yoko during the couple's avant-garde performance at Cambridge University's Mitchell Hall, while side two was recorded in their suite at London's Queen Charlotte Hospital, where Yoko was admitted with pregnancy complications, ultimately losing the baby.

I had no intention of buying it, let alone having any spare pocket money to purchase this bizarre record, but both my curiosity and loyalty were piqued when I read an item about it in *Disc and Music Echo*. This ended with a question to readers, along the lines of,

"Are you planning to buy this new John & Yoko album, and if so, why?" Along with the promise of sending free LP tokens as prizes for the six best answers.

Another Beatles-related competition! Naturally I wrote in straight away, not for a moment regarding the fact that I hadn't actually heard the album as an obstacle to winning another pop prize. What I wrote was basically complete twaddle, off the top of my head, but appeared reverential and heartfelt enough to possibly convince anyone that I'd bought the record and was positively affected by it.

In fact, 15 years later *Disc* editor Ray Coleman (later of *Melody Maker*) quoted part of my letter in his 1984 biography, *John Ono Lennon – Volume 2, 1967 – 1980*, as follows:

"Life With the Lions is a haunting, intriguing experience. Its pure concept is so refreshing and the sadness of the music – it is music – just makes me happy." Er, somehow I think not.

As you may have guessed, my winning letter was published, complete with my name and address, in the following week's edition of *Disc*. So imagine my surprise when I arrived home from school the following day, to find an envelope waiting for me on our hall table, having arrived that morning. My name and address had been written in scrawly black handwriting, which I vaguely recognised, but had no clue as to who it could be from.

On opening it, I was startled to find a black and white postcard of John and Yoko standing in front of the Eiffel Tower, taken on their honeymoon a couple of months earlier, along with their signatures. To say that I was well and truly gob-smacked would be an understatement. The realisation quickly set in that John had not only read my words of support in *Disc* on the day of publication, but had taken the time and trouble to immediately write and thank me personally, also writing the envelope himself.

This was quite remarkable, not just as a highly welcome gesture on his part, but also as a virtual admission that he and Yoko were extremely conscious of the overwhelming criticism of the record (and themselves), and were just thankful for any support they could muster. Incidentally, years later I happened to meet musician and songwriter Nick Laird-Clowes of the band Dream Academy (best known for 'Life in a Northern Town'), another lucky *Disc* winner whose letter was also published.

However, my delight at receiving this unique item of correspondence from John was to prove sadly short-lived, as, rather than follow Dad's good advice of putting it in the bank for safety, I stupidly took it with me in a small paper bag to the Blind Faith concert at Hyde Park held not long afterwards, to show to my pals ... and promptly lost it.

I absent-mindedly put the bag down beside me on the grass and completely forgot about it, so it was most likely picked up later along with all the other tons of rubbish. What a total plonker! If there's one thing that I regret losing it's that letter, although a few months later I did receive a form of compensation for it in a manner that was equally unexpected.

*

December 11, 1969 — exactly one year after the *Rock And Roll Circus* — marked the world premiere of *The Magic Christian* film, starring Peter Sellers and Ringo Starr, at the Odeon Kensington. The film was a vaguely satirical comedy, directed by Joe McGrath and loosely adapted from Terry Southern's 1959 novel. Luckily, it had an extremely catchy theme song, 'Come And Get It', performed by Badfinger but written by Paul McCartney, which for me was easily the best thing about this truly nonsensical movie.

Other stars appearing in cameo roles included John Cleese, Graham Chapman, Raquel Welch, Spike Milligan, Christopher Lee, Richard Attenborough, and Roman Polanski. I watched it again on television recently and to be honest it's a real mess, despite a few inspired moments. In my view it could easily have won a few Raspberry Awards if they'd existed back in the day.

However, the premiere was another challenge not to be missed. I duly travelled to High Street, Kensington with the full intention of trying to get myself into the big event, unlike the *Yellow Submarine* premiere the previous year, which had been more a mixture of spontaneity and good timing. This time I was on my own, but on seeing the large crowd outside the cinema I decided to bypass it by hailing a taxi from a short distance away, asking to be dropped outside the Odeon entrance.

A minute later, I was walking up the red carpet under a covered canopy along with other guests, mostly dressed in evening wear, while I would have been wearing a jacket, coat and scarf at that time of year. Everyone was bustling around the foyer, looking around to see who was there, while my mission was to try and get myself a seat for the big event. I approached the box office inside the cinema, to speak with a pleasant blue-rinsed lady, probably connected with the NSPCC (National Society for the Prevention of Cruelty to Children), the charity beneficiary of the premiere. I confidently explained to her,

"My aunt should have left my ticket here for collection,"

To which she replied,

"Alright dear, what name would that be under?"

Without batting an eyelid, I told her the name I'd decided upon just seconds earlier: don't ask me how or why, it just popped into my head.

"Benjamin Quincy-Jones," I quickly responded without missing a beat, not really having the slightest clue who Quincy was, but I'd obviously heard of him, and the name sounded important.

"I'm sorry love, but I can't see any tickets here under that name," the nice lady continued as she perused the list, "so I think you'll need to have a word with the organiser to sort things out *(sound familiar?)*. Actually, here she comes now," she continued, indicating behind me.

I quickly looked round, as a barrage of flashbulbs went off virtually in my face, and indeed spotted an extremely well-presented lady who was presumably the event organiser. The only problem being that she was, at that precise moment, walking in with the Queen's younger sister, Princess Margaret, Patron of the NSPCC and guest of honour at the premiere, along with her husband, Lord Snowdon. As I turned around, they were about to walk directly past me, followed by all the paparazzi, so the box office lady quickly said,

"Oh dear, you'd better not bother her now — here you are, take these," and hurriedly gave me a ticket and programme for the film.

Success, once again I was in.

However, the best was yet to come (yet again). As the royal party and others proceeded into the cinema, I spotted two familiar figures on the foyer steps, dressed all in black and holding a large placard proclaiming, *"Britain Murdered Hanratty"*, in large hand-written letters. It was John and Yoko, who at that moment were, rather surprisingly, standing together with nobody surrounding them, which presented the perfect opportunity for me.

I took my chance and walked up to ask them what it was all about, to which John explained that they were protesting on behalf of the family of the so-called 'A6 murderer'. James Hanratty had been executed in April 1962, aged just 25, one of the last people in the UK to receive capital punishment before it was abolished by Parliament. Although John and Yoko both seemed extremely focussed on their intent to proclaim Hanratty's innocence, there was actually another subject on my mind I wanted to express to John:

"I'd like to thank you for writing to me a few months ago, when I had my letter published in *Disc and Music Echo* in support of *Life With the Lions*." Well, what do you know — John said he remembered it, so I continued ...

"Actually, I do have one small confession to make, as I'd never heard the album before I wrote the letter, and still haven't to this day, to be honest."

Upon which both he and Yoko started laughing, saying they thought that was hilarious, and thanked me for my initiative. Sadly, I didn't have time to remind John about our encounters over the previous few years, but did have one more favour to ask him.

It was now time to go into the film, but not before I asked John to sign my souvenir programme, which featured Ringo and Peter Sellers on the cover, both of whom were also present that evening. He opened it at the third page, which sported a striking black and white portrait of Princess Margaret, taken by her husband. John promptly autographed it in blue ballpoint, just below the photograph but with an arrow pointing to the royal lips. A classic Lennon signature which still looks as though he'd signed it today, and a superb memento of another extraordinary occasion.

*

Just four nights later, on December 15 — actually after midnight on the 16th — John and George were on stage for a rare charity performance at the Lyceum Theatre on the Strand, billed as 'Peace for Christmas', in aid of UNICEF.

The Plastic Ono Band 'supergroup' for the occasion consisted of John and Yoko, George Harrison, Eric Clapton, Billy Preston, Klaus Voormann on bass, Alan White and Jim Gordon on drums, Delaney and Bonnie, Bobby Keys on sax, and Jim Price on trumpet. Keith Moon was also there, hitting White's floor-tom, while present but not performing were drummers Larry 'Legs' Smith of the Bonzos, and Dino Danelli of the Rascals.

And me? Well, I must have caught a cold at the premiere of *The Magic Christian*, as I was stuck home in bed and absolutely desolate that I was too unwell to attend the show. It would have been a very late night for me anyway, with getting home on public transport impossible at such a late hour. But I'm sure I would have made it there and back somehow, if I hadn't been struck down by the lurgy. However, my pal Jeff Dexter was present, and has shown me some of his private grainy black and white video of the event and backstage. It was also good that most of the show's audio recording was eventually included as the second disc on John and Yoko's *Sometime In New York City* album, released in 1972. But for me it was definitely the gig that got away, as well being the last Beatles-related show of the '60s.

WAR IS OVER!
IF YOU WANT IT

Love. John & Yoko

CHAPTER 8

LET IT BE

As the Swinging '60s ended, and the not-so swinging '70s dawned, it was fairly obvious that things in The Beatles' world were rapidly changing, with John the member who was becoming increasingly disenchanted with the group. From late '68 to early 1970, he released no less than four albums with Yoko: *Two Virgins, Life With The Lions, The Wedding Album*, and *Live Peace In Toronto*, plus two great Plastic Ono Band singles, 'Cold Turkey' and 'Instant Karma'. George had released two solo albums, *Wonderwall Music* and *Electronic Sound*, while Paul and Ringo were working on debut solo projects scheduled for release in the spring, *McCartney* and *Sentimental Journey* respectively.

I was still following their activities as much as ever, but had stopped adding to my scrapbooks, as their collective efforts slowed down considerably after *Abbey Road*, with only the prospect of the delayed release of the *Get Back* sessions and film to look forward to. Although John had privately told the rest of the group he was leaving back in September 1969, it wasn't until Paul announced his surprise departure on April 10, 1970 that the split became official.

A couple of months before the big news was announced publicly, I'd written to John at Apple, enclosing a portrait of him, printed from a lino cutting which I'd made in art class at school. It was subsequently published in the school magazine *Skylark*, which I conveniently happened to be joint editor of. I was quite proud of the print, and even more delighted when I received another reply from Peter Brown, dated February 18, 1970, again on 'Beatles & Co' headed paper, which read as follows:

"Dear David Stark, thank you for your letter of the 9th February. I confirm that I have passed on to John Lennon the magazine you enclosed. I regret that I cannot give you any positive information regarding Toronto as there are no confirmed details or dates at this time. The situation with the 'Get Back' premiere - one hopes it will be within the next few months, but again, there are no confirmed dates. Yours sincerely, Peter Brown."

I must have made reference in my letter to the release of the film version of John's *Live Peace in Toronto* concert the previous September, when he'd played with Eric Clapton, Klaus Voormann and Alan White. The album included great versions of such rock'n'roll classics as 'Blue Suede Shoes', 'Money' and 'Dizzy Miss Lizzy', alongside 'Yer Blues' and 'Cold Turkey', plus a side two scream-fest by Yoko. I'd also asked about the release of the much anticipated *Get Back* film, as it was originally titled, with Brown admitting his ignorance of the release plans for either project.

However, it was extremely nice of him to reply, and even nicer three months later, when out of the blue I received an official invitation from Apple for what was now re-titled *Let It Be,* the Beatles' fourth feature film, to be premiered at the London Pavilion on May 20, 1970.

I was extremely surprised and genuinely chuffed to be invited to what would be the final Beatles film premiere, especially after having bluffed my way into both *Yellow Submarine* and *The Magic Christian.* Our family had recently moved house, from Stanmore to Chestnut Avenue in nearby Edgware, and for some reason I pinned the invitation to a cork board on the kitchen wall, next to the telephone.

There it stayed for some weeks until the big day arrived, upon which, on removing it, I glanced at the reverse side and noticed that Mum had used it to write down a few items in pencil, which still survive today:

"Strawbs, bread, t/paste, baby oil, hand cream, cleaner."

Nice one, Mum — only you could write your shopping list on the back of a rare invitation from The Beatles and Apple.

Once again, I ventured to Piccadilly Circus with David Harris in tow for the big event, full of anticipation for another possible encounter with the Fab Four, or at least one or two of them. However, none of them turned up to the one Beatles premiere I was actually invited to. No big surprise though, as it would have been rather strange to see them in attendance, just a month after they'd officially split up. The words 'attending your own funeral' spring to mind.

However, Mary Hopkin, Lulu, Simon Dee, Spike Milligan and some members of the Stones and Fleetwood Mac were all there, although I can't remember exactly who we saw on the night. All in all, it was a rather subdued affair, particularly with the somewhat less than exciting, low-key Twickenham rehearsal scenes dominating much of the early action.

Thankfully, the Apple Studios section was a bit brighter, with the odd flashes of humour (mostly from Ringo), along with the welcome addition of Billy Preston on keyboards, which seemed to perk everyone up. The legendary rooftop finale also provided much-needed light relief, featuring a total of five songs: 'Get Back', 'Don't Let Me Down', 'I've Got a Feeling', 'One After 909' and 'Dig A Pony', three of which were re-taken once or twice. The 42-minute show concluded with their third attempt at 'Get Back', following which Lennon famously quipped,

"I'd like to say thank you on behalf of the group and ourselves and I hope we've passed the audition."

He and the other Beatles must surely have realised or decided at the time that this was to be their last-ever performance as a group. David and I left the cinema feeling slightly short-changed about the film, but at least we'd been there.

A mere half-century later, despite constant rumours of its reissue, *Let It Be* remains officially unreleased by Apple in any format. It now appears that it will form part of the forthcoming *Get Back* DVD package, which will also include a brand new, re-imagined version of the documentary, along with many out-takes, new interviews and other features. This was all painstakingly assembled by *Lord of the Rings* director, Peter Jackson, who was over in London to film some of the new interviews during 2019. The completed film was originally set for release in September 2020, but then moved back to August 2021 due to the Coronavirus pandemic.

Incidentally, a rather tenuous Beatles connection with Jackson is that, in 1967, the group were keen on starring in their own musical film version of *Lord of the Rings,* as at least John and Paul had been fans of J.R.R. Tolkien's trilogy since childhood. They even got as far as asking Stanley Kubrick to direct it, but he declined the offer. They also asked Tolkien to sell them the film rights, being promptly turned down flat, as the famous author and academic wasn't a big Beatles fan.

*

So, The Beatles had finally split up, and as some observers commented, the lavish *Let It Be* album box, complete with the glossy *Get Back* book, was somewhat reminiscent of a cardboard tombstone. Sadly, it was also far from their best album, despite some good tracks, with most fans feeling *Abbey Road,* recorded mostly a few months after *Let It Be,* was a far superior swan-song.

With the release of Paul's (mainly home-recorded) solo debut, *McCartney,* and Ringo's nostalgic *Sentimental Journey* released just a couple of weeks earlier, fans were slowly getting used to the fact that The Beatles were now four individual artists with very different aims and ambitions, as this challenging new decade established itself. Of course, John's original non-public decision to leave the group back in September '69; Paul's writ against the other three; and the band's ongoing financial wrangles all played a huge part in the break-up, but luckily they were all set on carving out solo careers for themselves, which would mean four times the output for the public to enjoy.

Speaking of Ringo, one Saturday night during the autumn of 1970, I was with my pal and bandmate Vince Lewis, trying to think of something different to do for the evening. We didn't fancy joining our usual bunch of friends at the Wimpy Bar by Edgware tube station. We didn't have much money and were dressed pretty scruffily.

Vince had recently bought his first car, a Ford Anglia, and for some unknown reason I came up with the crazy idea of driving a few miles to Hampstead to find Ringo's house and ask him out for a pint or two. Quite ridiculous I know, but that's what made it all the more a challenge. I knew the name of Ringo's street, which I'd probably seen mentioned in *The Beatles Book* monthly or elsewhere, but not the actual house number.

Compton Avenue turned out to be a secluded private road situated almost opposite the entrance of Kenwood House, a former stately home with enormous grounds on the posh side of Hampstead Heath. We parked on Spaniards Road, walked a few yards to our destination street and promptly rang the doorbell of the first house on the left, in order to ascertain the exact whereabouts of the Starkey residence.

However, we were somewhat taken aback when the door was quickly opened by none other than Scottish pop star Lulu, along with her then-husband, Maurice Gibb of the Bee Gees, who was wearing an apron — doing a bit of jive cooking on the side perhaps. They were obviously wondering what two young scruffs were doing on their doorstep on a Saturday evening, but couldn't have been nicer when I fibbed that we'd been invited to Ringo's place but weren't too sure which house it was.

"Oh, he's just down the end of the road on the right," said Lulu, nice as pie.

"You can't miss it," added Maurice, "It's got a big double drive. Give him our love as well."

Success! But could you imagine anyone, let alone a celebrity couple, giving that kind of private information about another celebrity to two complete strangers these days? We duly thanked them, said our goodbyes and walked a few yards down the road to find Ringo's large double-fronted house, named Round Hill, just as Maurice had described it. There was obviously some kind of party going on judging from the number of cars parked in and around the drive, but we mustered up some Dutch courage and rang the bell, then held our breath and waited.

We didn't have to wait long, as the door was opened by Ringo himself, casually dressed and holding a pool cue. He was obviously also wondering what the hell we were doing there.

"How can I help you, lads?" he asked.

"We were just wondering if you'd like to come out for a pint," I volunteered, feeling somewhat stupid but at least sticking to the plan.

"That's very nice of you, but I'm afraid we've got friends in tonight," Ringo replied, looking rather bemused but taking it all in his stride. "Another time maybe," he added.

As he said this, I suddenly spotted Eric Clapton walking through the hallway just a few feet behind him, so he wasn't just fobbing us off. We quickly said our goodbyes as Ringo closed the door, then off we headed up the street and back to the car, laughing our silly heads off. All great fun and definitely something a bit different to do on a boring Saturday night in north London.

*

The remainder of 1970 saw the release of two hugely important solo Beatles albums, commencing with George's *All Things Must Pass* in November. This majestic triple-album boxed set — actually two discs of new songs, plus the bonus extended 'Apple Jams' on the third — proved once and for all that George was a superb songwriter and artist in his own right. The set reached No. 1 in many countries around the world, and later went platinum in the USA, shipping over six million copies.

John Lennon/Plastic Ono Band quickly followed on December 11, proving to be a seminal and much-acclaimed work for John, despite failing to achieve quite the same level of chart success enjoyed by George. Interestingly, both albums were co-produced with Phil Spector but couldn't have been more different in style. While *All Things Must Pass* saw the top American producer (managed by Allen Klein) re-creating his legendary 1960s-style 'wall of sound' on many of George's tracks, John's angst-riddled album was one of the most basic and stripped-down ever to be released by a former Beatle.

I loved both records, playing them constantly in the run-up to Christmas, while other albums getting my attention at that time included Crosby, Stills, Nash & Young's *Déjà Vu*, *Led Zeppelin III*, *The Yes Album*, the Steve Miller Band's *Number 5*, and Peter Green's *The End of the Game*. I was also very much into cinema at the time, especially 'head' films such as *Woodstock, Gimme Shelter, Zabriskie Point*, and *Performance* (which I also attended the premiere of), as well as brilliant American comedy-dramas like *Little Big Man, Catch-22, Myra Breckenridge, M.A.S.H.*, and *Five Easy Pieces*.

I was still in my final year at school, studying for A-level exams in English, History and Art. As mentioned, we'd recently moved house, but things on the home front were beginning to break down, Dad having taken early retirement. He suffered a protracted nervous breakdown during the late '60s and was at home most days, causing severe problems between us all. Poor Mum had to put up with his many irrational outbursts, while Nigel and I also bore the brunt of his eccentricities and often-irrational behaviour, the atmosphere increasingly strained. It was an extremely difficult situation, especially for our lovely, kind and peace-loving mother, who eventually had to start divorce proceedings.

In complete frustration, I even bunked off school for a couple of days because of what was going on at home; it was definitely conflicting with my studies.

Around that time, thanks to an article I'd read in the *Daily Sketch*, I auditioned for a new pop music series being made for American TV, with auditions held at Pye Records near Marble Arch. *The Bugaloos* was a manufactured group, along the lines of The Monkees, but all living underground, like bugs, in their own little fantasy world.

Tragically, despite being all set on packing my bags for Hollywood, I was informed that I was too tall for the part, despite being on the short list (geddit?), but at least I did get my photo in the *Sketch*. As did sexy young actress Vicki Michelle, later of *'Allo 'Allo!* TV fame and a friend today, who also auditioned on the same day. The series, produced by Sid and Marty Krofft, ran for two seasons on NBC and was shown briefly in the UK but never quite took off in either country.

In hindsight, maybe that was the time when I should have chucked it all in, left school and tried my luck in the music business, or at least try and join a band on drums, not that I had enough experience at the time. Instead, I reluctantly went back to Habs and stuck it out until the A-level exams took place. I achieved B-grades in English and Art but flunked History. So, no university for me then, which I wasn't too worried about, despite having no real idea as to which direction I was heading after saying a final farewell to school at the end of June 1971.

But just as I left school, someone else was planning to leave the country for distant shores abroad, not that we had any idea about this at the time, or how it would eventually work out.

*

The last time I ever set eyes on John Lennon was on July 15, 1971, when he and Yoko were at Selfridges to sign copies of Yoko's re-published *Grapefruit* book, just weeks before the couple left England for New York. The publicly-advertised event in Oxford Street resulted in a heavily-crowded signing session at the famous store, but with very little of the heavy security found at similar events these days.

John and Yoko were seated at a table, surrounded by hordes of fans gawping and taking photos of them from all sides. The event was being overseen by various Selfridges staffers and representatives from Sphere Books, Yoko's publisher. John was wearing a dark jacket over a yellow *Grapefruit* T-shirt, obviously keen on demonstrating his full support for the new paperback edition of his wife's avant-garde collection of thoughts (aka 'pieces') and drawings, first published in 1964, some two years before the couple met. Meanwhile, Yoko was looking rather sexy in a floral hot-pants outfit, and sporting a black beret.

I dutifully bought a copy of the small, square and red-covered book for just 40p. It was also priced as eight shillings in old money, as the signing took place exactly five months after Great Britain went decimal on February 15, 1971, with goods still marked up in both systems of currency. After reaching the front of the queue, I was able to get the book signed by John and Yoko, also trying to exchange a few quick words with them in the scrum. The scene was totally chaotic as you can imagine, and while I later regretted not buying more than one copy, as some others did, I was more than pleased to see the couple again, not knowing that within a month John would be leaving England permanently to settle down in New York with Yoko.

Two postscripts: Firstly, while researching this section I googled the book-signing and found a few images online. These included one of the crowd surrounding John and Yoko, in which I can just be seen in the top right corner. I'd never seen that particular photo before, but what a great find. Secondly, John and Yoko held another signing session the following day, at Claude Gill bookshop, also on Oxford Street. I didn't make it to this one, but two of my school pals did, Paul Levett and also David Kent, who got lucky in managing to get a couple of pictures with John.

*

After John and Yoko's move to New York on August 31, 1971, my Beatle encounters slowed down quite considerably, not only because The Beatles were all pursuing separate careers, but also because, having now left school, I needed to start work at some point. But before then, I enjoyed a few weeks' vacation, including a week in Paris with pals David Harris and future Mud Club legend Philip Sallon, with the total cost being a mere £12 each, including the ferry over. Philip's legendary social networking skills were evident even then, as I don't know anyone else of 18 years old who could have bumped into someone they knew at the top of the Eiffel Tower.

On our return I started job-hunting, and with luck found a suitable position almost straight away. I became assistant to the promotions manager at Premier Drums, based at the company's small London office suite on Regent Street. Being an aspiring drummer myself, I was more than delighted to be working for the UK's top percussion brand and meeting endorsees of the company's products, such as John Coghlan of Status Quo; Rob Townsend of Family; and — top of the bill — Keith Moon, backstage at the Rainbow Theatre in Finsbury Park, when The Who famously launched it with three nights of concerts in November 1971.

I had briefly met Moonie a couple of times before, at the Marquee Club and the Saville Theatre, which unsurprisingly he didn't remember, but was polite enough, if somewhat brief, when I met him backstage with Paul Levett. The fact that he had attractive female company in the dressing room with him might have had something to do with the brevity of our meeting, but it was great to see him again. The job at Premier was proving perfect for me, while I also had to attend a few jazz gigs in my new professional capacity, meeting such names as Kenny Clare, Kenny Clarke, and American drum maestro Louie Bellson.

All was going extremely well work-wise until a week or two after the Rainbow shows, when my boss Graham Morley suddenly informed me that the company would be closing the London office by the end of the year, which naturally stunned me. He offered me the opportunity of relocating to Wigston, near Leicester, where the company's factory and main offices were located. However, I politely declined, despite also being asked by managing director Fred Della-Porter to stay on. I enjoyed working at Premier but knew it wouldn't be quite the same in Wigston. I'd been there once in order to visit the factory, but that was quite enough, thank you very much.

This bolt from the blue wasn't at all part of my career plan, so in early 1972 I had to rethink things and start again. However, this time I ended up working rather closer to home than expected. Our parents' divorce was imminent, and Mum was flat-hunting for herself, Nigel and I. We lived in a couple of short-stay apartments for a while, before settling at the appropriately-named Nigel Court, a brand-new block in Finchley Central.

By then I'd become somewhat disheartened by the sudden end of my budding music industry career, so when the manager of the local estate agents who sold us the flat mentioned that they had an opening for a junior negotiator, I took the job.

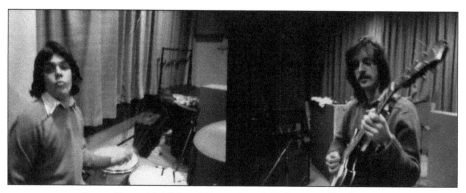

Recording with Richard Rangeley of Riviera Feedback, 1975.

CHAPTER 9

ONLY A NORTHERN SONG

For the next 18 months, I became a rookie estate agent, showing prospective clients around flats and houses in north London, which in those days started at around £15,000 or even less. If only I'd been able to afford a place for myself at that time, however small. Nigel and I were still living at home and both working, with Mum forced to get a job for the first time since before her marriage. For a while, she ran a ceramics shop in Hampstead, before working in customer relations at Rediffusion TV Rentals' showroom by Piccadilly Circus – just minutes from where I had worked at Premier Drums.

However, my budding property career did have its occasional perks, such as when the company was appointed by Spike Milligan to sell his house in North Finchley and arrange the purchase of his impressive new one, named Monkenhurst, in Hadley Wood, near Barnet. On telling him I lived in Finchley Central, he immediately quipped,

"Ah yes, a much better class of vandalism there!"

Apart from mentioning my somewhat distant relationship to Peter Sellers, I also informed Spike that I was born at the same hospital and around the same time as his daughter Laura, thanks to Mum recalling that she was in the same ward as Spike's wife Shelagh.

Meanwhile, in 1972 I was also playing drums with my first band, Raw Deal, with Dave Kent on lead vocals and organ; Andy Leigh on guitar; and Vince Lewis on bass and vocals. We formed the band the previous year, and played occasional gigs in north London and Hertfordshire. We also rehearsed on a regular basis at a paintbrush factory owned by Andy's family, situated on the A1 in Boreham Wood — hardly ideal acoustically, but at least a free space to practise, where we could also store our gear.

Our repertoire consisted of some good original songs, mostly written by Dave, plus covers of The Allman Brothers Band, The Doobie Brothers, The Doors, The Eagles, and even Alice Cooper, a fairly mixed bag of material with a US bias. But funnily enough no Beatles songs, although I think we may have murdered 'Get Back' a few times.

In early 1973, Paul McCartney announced plans for a one-hour TV special, *James Paul McCartney*, following the completion of Wings' second album, *Red*

Rose Speedway. The ATV production would feature a mix of video and location sequences, as well as a concert section in front of an invited audience, to be filmed at Elstree Studios in Boreham Wood on Sunday, March 18.

That happened to be the same day Raw Deal would be rehearsing in the paintbrush factory, a mere 10 minutes' drive away. So, despite the slightly inconvenient but totally irrelevant lack of tickets for the show, fellow Beatles fan Dave Kent and I made the short trip to Elstree Studios after our band session. We parked up, then just had to decide on the best course of action, as the audience was already inside the studio, ready and waiting for Wings' performance.

Luckily, we didn't have to think too long, for as we wandered around the perimeter of the building, I spotted a huge studio door left slightly ajar. A few seconds later we were inside and mingling with the crowd, who were mostly sitting on the floor waiting for the show to begin. Talk about good timing: we sat down in the middle of the audience and didn't have to wait long before Paul and the band took to the stage to play a short selection of recent songs: 'Little Woman Love', 'C Moon', 'My Love' and 'The Mess', along with 'Maybe I'm Amazed'.

This was our first chance to see Paul's new group, who had already played a short try-out tour of UK universities the previous year, followed by a full European tour, but hadn't officially played anywhere in the London area before now. Apart from Paul and Linda McCartney, the line-up consisted of Denny Laine (ex-Moody Blues) and Henry McCullough (ex-Grease Band) on guitars, plus US session musician Denny Seiwell on drums. They were all on top form, inspiring the audience to get up on its feet right away. I particularly enjoyed the extended version of 'The Mess', the B-side of recent single 'My Love', a superb, timeless Macca ballad which was played perfectly, including Henry's memorable guitar solo. I rather think he'd have been sacked on the spot by Paul if it hadn't been.

It was exciting to be there, especially as we'd sneaked in for free, and we looked forward to seeing the finished TV show on May 10, nearly a month after its US airing on April 16. Unfortunately, the critics weren't too kind, Paul getting slated for overdoing the schmaltz in various sequences. The overall result was somewhat disjointed, and in some places rather insipid, as one brutal commentator put it, although to be fair the live concert section was anything but that.

One sequence, which attracted particular panning for its syrupy overtones, was a video performance of Paul's most recent single, 'Mary Had a Little Lamb', with the band dressed in white shirts and trousers, all set in a dreamy field and lake sequence by a rustic bridge.

By coincidence, Dave and I knew that bridge extremely well, as it was located in a picturesque area known as Tyke's Water, by our old school grounds in nearby Elstree. The same spot was used as a location over the years for many other programmes, such as *The Avengers, Danger Man, The Saint*, and even a *Dracula* film. I have great memories of seeing Patrick Macnee and Diana Rigg (aka John Steed and Emma Peel of *The Avengers*) driving in Steed's vintage Bentley down the school drive, in pursuit of a fully-costumed Cybernaut.

I also met Patrick McGoohan on the set of *Danger Man* at school in 1965 and obtained his autograph. Some 30 years later, I met him again while boarding a plane at LAX (Los Angeles Airport), this time getting a photo with him as well as another signature. Also in the queue was famous restaurateur Michael Chow, who informed McGoohan that he'd been an extra in *The Prisoner*, my all-time favourite TV series.

So it was quite a surprise, but also somewhat ironic, to see an ex-Beatle singing his soppy children's song in the very spot where we and our fellow schoolmates would often sneak off to at lunchtime for a discreet smoke. Although the TV special was slightly disappointing, Paul was back at what he was best doing a couple of weeks after it was screened.

On May 25, I returned to Hammersmith Odeon with brother Nigel, for Wings' first official London show, part of their nationwide tour to promote *Red Rose Speedway*. Naturally, Paul was greeted with all the usual hysteria that an ex-Beatle could muster, especially as he was now much more confident about playing Wings numbers plus a few of his solo efforts. But unlike his shows these days, not a single Beatles-related song in sight apart from an encore of Little Richard's 'Long Tall Sally' that brought the house down each night. It was great to see Wings for the second time in two months, but the shorter, much more intimate set at Elstree Studios remains the one which lingers in my memory from that period.

Playing live gigs and rehearsing with Raw Deal took up a lot more of my time and energy, making my property career increasingly less interesting to me as 1973 turned into '74. Despite having a small company car and earning a reasonable salary, I'd realised that being an estate agent wasn't really for me, so I decided that I had to somehow try and get back into the music business, despite a lack of suitable contacts.

That was until a pal of mine mentioned one day that his cousin was married to the son of Dick James (him again), who, after his incredible success with The Beatles, was now flying high as publisher of Elton John, now a world superstar. Dick was of course the person who inadvertently helped me out at the *Yellow Submarine* premiere six years earlier.

My first thought was that Dick James Music (DJM) might be a potential opportunity for Raw Deal's music. I made an appointment to see Dick's son, Stephen James, on the basis that I had a demo tape to play him. Even as I sat down in his office on New Oxford Street, I knew it was a lost cause, as a very rough cassette recorded in a paintbrush factory, along with some horrible echo, wasn't exactly going to set the world or DJM Records alight. It only took a few moments for Stephen to turn it off, informing me that there wasn't much he could do with it.

However, in our ensuing conversation, he mentioned that there was a job going in the company which he could offer me, if I was prepared to start from the bottom. I'd already written to a few other companies, such as EMI, Decca and Pye but hadn't heard back, so, weighing up the odds, I thought it would be a good chance to get into the business, even in a lowly capacity. DJM was a well-respected organisation, encompassing records, music publishing, an artist agency, and its own recording studio, so I duly accepted Stephen's offer.

I began working there a couple of weeks later and was soon running around town delivering tapes, promo records and other urgent items, mainly for the in-house studio or the press office. Elton John occasionally visited the building in his chauffeured brown Rolls Royce, 'Hercules' inscribed on the wing. I recall him coming in and throwing telephones around the reception area in his early tantrum days, but always with a grin on his face and a laugh. I was a big fan by then, and could also relate to him as he came from Pinner, just up the road from Stanmore.

Elton and DJM enjoyed huge success with the double-album *Goodbye Yellow Brick Road*, released the year before, while in 1974 the follow-up, *Caribou* was another No.1 record, including the smashes 'The Bitch Is Back' and 'Don't Let The Sun Go Down On Me', an incredible song which I absolutely loved.

Other top songwriters signed to DJM at the time included Roger Cook and Roger Greenaway; Chris Arnold, David Martin and Geoff Morrow; Ron Roker, and Moon Williams. I also occasionally hung out with producer Phil Wainman and his partner, David Walker, who successfully worked with The Sweet and Bay City Rollers, and who were then working with their old pal Johnny Goodison on a project under the name of Big John's Rock 'N' Roll Circus (wonder where they got that idea from).

On one occasion, I bumped into one of Dick's former songwriter clients on the steps of Abbey Road Studios, as I arrived to pick up or deliver a tape. It was Paul McCartney, who on my telling him I was now working at Dick James Music, looked at me with a rather surprised expression, merely saying,

"OK, good luck with that then."

The reason for his cool response being that, in 1969, Dick controversially sold his shares in Northern Songs to Lew Grade's ATV empire without telling John or Paul. Even five years on, there was still little love lost on the ex-Beatle's part.

Meanwhile, Elton's incredible early '70s success was very much DJM's saving grace around which everything else revolved, such as one-hit wonders like Mr. Bloe's 'Groovin' With Mr. Bloe', while other artist signings included Danny Kirwan (ex-Fleetwood Mac), Ireland's Horslips, Johnny Guitar Watson, and actor Dennis Waterman.

I found Dick to be a genial kind-hearted character, and although I never got to know him well, I respected him as the founder of a musical empire I was pleased to be part of, if only for a very short time. After just a few weeks of employment

I received a letter from Decca Records, requesting my presence for an interview with international manager Marcel Stellman; another music business legend, for whom I started working in September 1974.

*

I did have one other Beatle encounter during my brief time at DJM, when I heard that George Harrison was going to be interviewed by 'Little' Nicky Horne on his early evening Capital Radio programme, *Your Mother Wouldn't Like It*. It was quite a surprise, as George had no new record out at that time. His next album, *Dark Horse* wouldn't be released until December. I went along after work to Capital's studios at Euston Tower, expecting that George would come out directly after the interview. Which indeed he did, accompanied by American saxophonist Tom Scott, who was recording with him at the time.

The so-called 'quiet Beatle' was in a very friendly mood, possibly as there were only a couple of other people there. We chatted for quite a while, before someone produced a camera and we all lined up for a group shot, George with ciggy in hand. Many years later, I received an email from the girl standing between George and myself, which I've managed to lose, so if you're reading this, please do get back in touch.

I was fortunate to meet George again one month later in rather different circumstances, by which time I was doing international press and promotions at Decca. As mentioned, Mum was working at Rediffusion TV Rentals, and one day was asked to provide a television set for the London flat of Ravi Shankar, the celebrated Indian composer, musician, and lifelong friend and mentor of George Harrison.

The call came from someone at George's office, which was paying for the rental, who mentioned that Mr. Shankar would be playing a concert at the Royal Albert Hall the following week, and would Mrs. Stark like a couple of complimentary tickets? Well, Mrs. Stark was always up for new and interesting musical experiences, so she graciously accepted the very generous offer, and off we both went.

The concert took place on Monday, September 23, our seats located in the Albert Hall's stalls, opposite the stage on the far side of the auditorium. As the lights went down, George walked on stage to introduce Ravi, who'd recently signed to Harrison's Dark Horse Records, the album *Shankar Family & Friends* released just three days earlier. You can see video footage of this introduction on YouTube, with George wearing a long-sleeved yellow Dark Horse T-shirt.

A few minutes after George left the stage and the concert had begun, I heard shuffling behind us, and looked round in astonishment to see George taking his seat directly behind ours. This seemed quite extraordinary, until it dawned on me that his office had given us VIP seats in the same vicinity, a very nice gesture indeed. We waited until the interval before we were able to speak, when I reminded him we'd met outside Capital Radio just a few weeks earlier. I was also proud to introduce Mum to him as the lady from Rediffusion who'd provided Ravi with his TV set - essential information that I'm sure impressed George no end.

George seemed to be on his own that evening, as he was quite happy to chat with us, before excusing himself to go to the bar or loo. It was quite something to see him talking with Mum, who took this unexpected encounter completely in her stride, the two of them getting on famously. Ever discreet, Mum later went on to work as PA to an eminent Harley Street doctor and mental health pioneer, Robin Skynner, who co-wrote a book with John Cleese. He also had other celebrity patients, about whom Mum would never say a word to Nigel or myself.

However, it was after George re-took his seat and the Shankar concert continued for the second half that the totally unexpected happened. I have to confess that, despite my appreciation of being there, Indian music has never been quite my cup of Darjeeling, and although Mum was enjoying it rather more than I was, I heard her whispering to me towards the end of the show,

"I think we should start making a move soon, darling."

True to form, she was thinking about our long tube journey home, rightly bearing in mind that we both had to be back in town for work the next day. But just as we were gathering our things and getting ready to leave, I felt a hand on my shoulder as George leaned over to say,

"You can't leave yet, the best bit's just coming up."

I still have absolutely no idea what the 'best bit' actually was, but of course we stayed right to the end by royal ex-Beatle command, before saying our goodbyes to George after the show finally concluded. And I still have my copy of the beautiful souvenir programme, which I never asked him to sign. Doh...

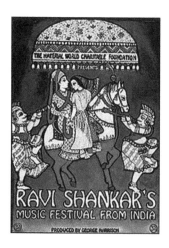

CHAPTER 10

THE DECCA TAPES

The mid-'70s were less about The Beatles and more about me getting on with my career at Decca. I was now working with, among others, The Moody Blues on their various solo releases at that time, most notably Justin Hayward and John Lodge's wonderful *Blue Jays* album and single 'Blue Guitar'. I was kept busy setting up interviews with European journalists for them and other members of the band, who were going in the same solo direction as The Beatles but only for a couple of years. On one occasion, I was snapped in a photo with their singer and flautist Ray Thomas, used in a Norwegian magazine article to promote his album *From Mighty Oaks*.

One memorable trip involved spending three days in Hamburg with John Entwistle of The Who, plugging his *Mad Dog* album, as recorded by 'John Entwistle's Ox' and released by Decca. That was a real treat for me, as he was happy to answer pretty much everything I wanted to know about The Who and relate all the infamous stories, mostly involving Moonie. I only wish I could have taped our conversations during the flights and during our stay in Hamburg, as he certainly didn't hold anything back. A very dry-humoured guy and a superb bass player, as well as being an excellent caricaturist of the band.

I met John quite a few times over the years, but had a huge shock when I was in Las Vegas in late June 2002, as a guest for The Who's summer tour launch at the Hard Rock Hotel. Tragically, the intimate gig for 300 press and media folk never happened, as John had gone and snuffed it the night before, in true rock'n'roll style. If only I'd met up with my friends Bob and Kathy at the Hard Rock that night instead of going to a House of Blues gig: I'm sure I would have seen The Ox holding court in the bar. But it wasn't to be. Instead, I spent the following morning commiserating with fellow fan Peter Frampton at a Vegas art gallery, where John should have been the guest of honour to launch a special exhibition of his drawings and prints.

*

The legendary Dick Rowe was a senior member of Decca's A&R department, and still working at the company while I was there, although our paths didn't cross too often. However, I was rather keen to speak to him about his memories of famously turning down The Beatles, after they auditioned at Decca's studios in Broadhurst Gardens, West Hampstead on January 1, 1962.

Better known now as the Decca Tapes, the 15 tracks the group recorded that New Year's Day (not a public holiday then) included three original Lennon/ McCartney songs which ironically later became hits for other artists: 'Hello Little Girl', covered by The Fourmost; 'Like Dreamers Do' by The Applejacks; and 'Love of The Loved', Cilla Black's debut single. The remaining 12 songs were ones they played many times on stage, of which 'Money' and 'Till There Was You' were the only two to eventually be re-recorded and officially released by the group, as later included on *With The Beatles*.

So the group's audition performance actually included a handful of songs that would become big money-spinners for them within the next couple of years, as either writers or performers. Easy to say in hindsight, but who could possibly have known at that time how big they would become apart from manager Brian Epstein, with his unwavering faith in the group's writing and performing talents.

Decades later we learned, thanks to Mark Lewisohn's meticulous research in *Tune In*, that Epstein and The Beatles were apparently offered the opportunity of having their audition tape released as an independently-produced album, but only if they paid the sum of £100 for the pleasure. Epstein refused on principle, so in effect he and the group actually turned Decca down, and not the other way round.

I didn't know any of this when, sometime during 1975, I asked Dick if he fancied having lunch together, which we did in the Decca executive canteen one day — a rare privilege for me at that time. Sadly, I have scant recollection of our conversation, or even what we ate, but I do recall Dick talking about Brian Poole & the Tremeloes, who auditioned for Decca on the same day as The Beatles.

Dick's right-hand man, Mike Smith, wanted to sign both groups, having seen them play live, until Dick told him that they could only sign one. According to *Tune In*, Smith famously favoured the Tremeloes for various reasons: they were based in south-east London (in Dagenham, near where Smith lived in Barking) and had better and more expensive gear; and were in general the more organised group. Plus, Smith's optician had originally tipped him off about the group, as he was managing them at the time, so there was slight nepotism involved as well.

So Brian Poole & the Tremeloes were duly signed, while The Beatles and Epstein walked away from Decca. However, as luck would have it, it was George Harrison who later tipped Dick Rowe off, when they were both judging a talent contest in Liverpool, about a great rhythm and blues band he'd seen by the name of the Rolling Stones. No dithering this time, as the Stones were quickly signed by Decca in May 1963, just days after Dick saw them play at the Crawdaddy Club in Richmond.

Dick Rowe left Decca later in 1975, so I feel extremely pleased to have had that lunch with him, and I'm sure we must have discussed some of the many other acts he either signed or produced for the label. These included The Moody Blues, The Zombies, Them with Van Morrison, John Mayall's Bluesbreakers, The Tornados, The Bachelors, Tom Jones, Billy Fury, Tommy Steele, and Cat Stevens.

Sadly, Dick died in 1986 from diabetes-related causes, while his colleague Mike Smith passed away in 2011.

*

The year 1975 also saw the launch of a major new Decca signing, Newcastle-born singer-songwriter John Miles, whose excellent singles, 'Music' and 'Highfly', among others on the label, helped revive the company's somewhat sagging chart fortune at that time. John is a nice easy-going guy, whom I accompanied to Europe for TV appearances. I was also privileged to be one of the first people to hear 'Music', well before its release date. The track was played for me by John's manager, Cliff Cooper, on huge studio monitors at his Orange Studio and offices in Denmark Street. I was totally impressed at the time, and have loved the Alan Parsons-produced record ever since; a real pop/classical opus if ever there was one.

Other artists I worked with at Decca included 10cc, Camel, Gilbert O'Sullivan, Peter Skellern, Morris Albert, Gilbert Becaud, Typically Tropical, Caravan, and Curved Air. Plus, indirectly, the Rolling Stones, whose back-catalogue was still under Decca control, following the band's departure to form Rolling Stones Records in 1970. It seemed like there was a new Stones compilation put out by Decca every few months, the best being the double-album *Rolled Gold*, released in 1975.

I was kept extremely busy by my boss, Marcel Stellman, who apart from being a brilliant multi-lingual promotions man, was also a record producer, prolific lyricist and song translator himself. He wrote the English lyrics for 'Tulips From Amsterdam', as well as songs for Petula Clark, Charles Aznavour, Les Paul & Mary Ford, and Nina Simone, among others. Years later, after leaving Decca when it was acquired by Polygram, Marcel picked up the UK rights to a popular French TV quiz show, *Des Chiffres et des Lettres,* as he thought it could also work well in the UK. The show was retitled *Countdown* for British audiences, and nearly 40 years after its launch in 1982 – as the first programme screened on Channel 4 - it's still going strong. In fact, it's become the longest-running British quiz show of all time, with Marcel credited at the end of every edition.

He's 95 now and we're still good friends, while one legendary single many don't realise Marcel produced was The Goons' 'Ying Tong Song', coupled with 'I'm Walking Backwards for Christmas', both recorded in 1956. Most people think

George Martin produced these titles for EMI, but no, although he did work later with The Goons on other occasions.

In 2011, I took what is the only known photograph of the two Goons producers pictured together, at the Savoy Hotel for BASCA's annual Gold Badge Awards lunch, where Sir George was being honoured for his outstanding career. Marcel and I jokily welcomed him to 'the club', having both received our own Gold Badges by then.

*

Back on the band front, Raw Deal split up in early 1975, so Dave Kent and I formed a new group with singer/guitarist Martin Coslett, lead guitarist Richard Rangeley and bassist John Pooley. We called ourselves Riviera Feedback, named after Richard's Epiphone Riviera guitar, which at one point had been making some extremely weird feedback sounds. As well as playing local gigs, we also ventured to The University of Surrey in Guildford, which had an eight-track studio; quite a rarity on campus back then.

We recorded two sets of demos in 1975 and '76, a mix of originals written by Dave and Martin, as well as one of mine. Sadly, the tapes got no further, but I did get them both cut as 12-inch acetates, sending the masters over to Decca's extremely obliging transcription department.

Later, during the blistering heatwave of July 1976, we played our most high-profile gig, as support to Eddie & the Hot Rods the night they recorded their famous *Live at The Marquee* EP. It was the only time we played London's most revered rock venue, with Vince Lewis replacing John on bass for the occasion.

Somehow, I managed to secure the gig with relative ease, but it was only years later when the reason for this became apparent. I read somewhere that the Hot Rods dumped their previous support act at the Marquee Club, as they'd smashed up some of the Rods' gear onstage. That band's name — maybe no surprise here — was the Sex Pistols. So we were chosen as a safe bet for the night, our melodic rock providing a marked contrast to the Pistols, who I'd actually seen with pals at one of their infamous 100 Club shows just a few weeks earlier. They were a rowdy lot, with no obvious talent apparent to us that night, as it was all attitude and gobbing. But I later grew to love the classic *Never Mind the Bollocks* album.

Meanwhile, the Marquee was packed out and sweltering for our support slot to the Hot Rods, during the blazing hot summer of '76. Even Mum and her future second husband Leonard, plus Nigel, came down and braved the stifling heat, along with the rambunctious, beer-swilling punk crowd. I still have some photos of our set taken by old pal David Jacobs, the rabbi's son from the Brian Epstein memorial service.

One postscript: in 2013, I met John Lydon (aka Johnny Rotten) at the launch for the annual BMI London Awards, held at the Dorchester Hotel, where he was being honoured as a 'BMI Icon' (true). I told him the story of how Riviera Feedback came to support the Hot Rods instead of the Pistols, at which he laughed and said in his inimitable sneering style,

"You got our gig!"

*

August 1976 marked my first visit of many to the United States, flying on Laker Airways to JFK airport, New York with Vince Lewis. We stayed in a Manhattan YMCA for a couple of nights, and also met up at the Empire State Building with fellow tourists Dave Kent, his sister Mandy and David Jacobs, who were all visiting at the same time. It was great fun to be with good friends during our first time in the Big Apple, where we did all the sights before Vince and I moved on for a fun-packed two-week trip by Greyhound Bus, taking in Washington, Orlando, Nashville and Boston, among other locations.

I'd also pre-arranged two complimentary tickets, via MCA Records, for Elton John's show at Madison Square Garden on August 17, with special guest Kiki Dee, a spectacular night. Vince has since reminded me that, before show-time, we spent an hour outside the venue trying to sell our free tickets for $100 each.

Apparently, the highest offer was only $50, so I'm rather pleased that in the end we put Elton's performance over our poverty. Especially as he included his version of 'Lucy In The Sky With Diamonds' during the show, which made me wish I'd been at the Garden two years earlier, when John Lennon famously joined him to sing it, along with 'Whatever Gets You Through The Night' and 'I Saw Her Standing There'.

Vince also assures me that, not only did we visit the Dakota Building, but on arrival had a few words with the doorman, who buzzed through to the Lennons' apartment to announce our presence. We then spoke directly with Yoko on the intercom, who told us that no, John wasn't in and we couldn't come up. I'm guessing that I must have told the doorman I'd met the couple before, and that I also worked in the music business. On reflection it's quite possible that if I'd taken the trouble to write to John in advance, and remind him of our previous encounters, we might have had better luck.

*

Back in Blighty, Paul McCartney had returned to the road in a big way with the massive year-long *Wings Over the World* tour, which started in the UK in September 1975. The tour included two nights at Hammersmith Odeon, concluding a year later with three nights at Wembley's Empire Pool in October 1976. This was when the band was at its finest in my opinion, with masterful playing by Paul, Denny Laine and Jimmy McCulloch, together with new addition

Joe English on drums, a superb player. Plus, Tony Dorsey, Howie Casey, Thaddeus Richard and Steve Howard on saxes, brass and percussion; and last but not least, the lovely Linda on keyboards and backing vocals.

I remember the Wembley show for all the wrong reasons, as I'd driven there and parked the car some distance away. On returning to the spot after the show it was nowhere to be found, having been stolen. Fortunately though, it turned up a few days later in a somewhat soggy state but luckily undamaged.

Meanwhile, Riviera Feedback split up in early 1977, after which I joined a short-lived faux-punk band, the Blood Group, featuring guitarist and songwriter Joe Kerr, who later went on to work with Thomas Dolby, co-writing 'She Blinded Me With Science'; and his brother Tim, who's now Sir Timothy and a High Court judge. I'd also found a great lead singer by the name of Charlie Fawn, a good-looking version of Sid Vicious, leather-clad and with a terrific voice, who later had a few solo records released on Arista Records.

We only played a handful of gigs, supporting bands like The Lurkers at the Red Cow in West Kensington, and Racing Cars (of 'They Shoot Horses Don't They?' fame) at a May Ball in Oxford, a lot of drunken fun for all the students attending in evening wear and for us. We also recorded a few tracks in a Soho studio, including a couple of mine, both tongue-in-cheek pot-shots at punk culture, 'Second Class Juvenile' and 'Everybody Looks The Same' - which they mostly did.

Charlie also sang backing vocals on another of my efforts, 'Who Are The Mysterons?', a sci-fi/punk epic sung by Gideon Wagner and recorded at Morgan Studios in Willesden Green, along with my sci-fi comedy number 'Robot Romance'. Both tracks featured top session drummer Clem Cattini of The Tornados, who I didn't know at the time but has since become a good pal. Clem's the man with some of the funniest studio and session stories, along with bassist Mo Foster, another good friend and neighbour.

By that time, I'd moved on from Decca after being approached by MAM Records, a division of Management, Agency and Music Ltd., owned by the late Gordon Mills, who managed Tom Jones, Engelbert Humperdinck and Gilbert O'Sullivan. These three stars were all released through Decca, so it was just a short hop away for me, job-wise, but maybe not the best move of my career, due mainly to old-style management.

I became much more interested in the company's concert division, which promoted shows by the likes of Frank Sinatra, Barry Manilow, and Liza Minelli. This led me to work on many of the souvenir programmes sold at such prestigious shows, produced by a nearby specialist company which I later joined, with free concert tickets usually thrown in as well. This became my introduction to eventually working on various music trade publications; editing studio magazines and compiling industry directories, which over the next few years became my main work.

*

It was three years until Wings' next tour of the UK, which started in November 1979 to promote the *Back to the Egg* album, including London dates at Lewisham Odeon and the Rainbow Theatre. Plus, four nights at Wembley Arena, where I also saw support act and pal Earl Okin playing his unique brand of jazz and bossa nova for the first time. The tour eventually culminated in Paul's headline appearance in the *Concert for Kampuchea* at Hammersmith Odeon on December 29.

Tickets to that show were like gold-dust, but luckily I had a very good connection, managing to see The Who, Queen, Ian Dury & the Blockheads, The Pretenders, The Clash, and The Specials play that week, with everyone on top form. As was also the case on the big finale night, opened by Elvis Costello & the Attractions along with Nick Lowe's Rockpile, plus special guest Robert Plant. Then followed a full set by Wings, before the mighty 'Rockestra' super-group hit the stage, featuring Paul and Linda, Pete Townshend, David Gilmour, Dave Edmunds, Denny Laine, Laurence Juber, John Paul Jones, John Bonham, Gary Brooker, Ronnie Lane, Kenney Jones, and others.

Paul and the band opened (and closed) their set with the thunderous 'Rockestra Theme', followed by 'Let It Be', before they ripped into a rocking great version of Little Richard's 'Lucille'. A top night to end a sensational week of shows, all staged to benefit the people of war-torn Cambodia, thousands of whom were the victims of tyrannical dictator Pol Pot.

We didn't know it then, but this was to be Paul's final concert performance until an even bigger charity event six years later, namely *Live Aid* in July 1985. However, as the new decade dawned, there was big trouble looming for Paul on the other side of the world, while the first year of the 1980s ended with the totally unimaginable happening to John, right outside his New York home.

CHAPTER 11

NOTHING IS REAL

The year 1980 was a troubled one from the start in Beatle-world. Paul was arrested in January for possession of marijuana on his arrival in Japan, subsequently spending nine days in a Tokyo prison cell, causing Wings' planned tour there to be abandoned. Meanwhile, Ringo was concentrating on his film acting career, in such international blockbusters as *Caveman,* while George's autobiography, *I Me Mine* was published in August, the first of many beautifully-designed books from Genesis Publications, the author strangely paying scant reference to John Lennon's influence on his life within its pages.

However, the big news later that summer was that John had returned to the recording studio for the first time in five years, working on a new album with Yoko, eventually revealed as *Double Fantasy.* It was set for release on November 17, preceded by the single '(Just Like) Starting Over' on October 24, two days before my 28th birthday.

It was a rather strange experience to hear the single previewed on Capital Radio a few days earlier, as it was obviously a brand new Lennon song but with a rather ironic late '50s feel to it, plus some unexpected female backing vocals: this was John referencing his musical past but also telling us that he was back, and feeling optimistic about the future. I liked it on first hearing and couldn't wait to hear the album when it arrived — the only downside being that when it did, John's tracks were interspersed with Yoko's, which was annoying at the time, although I respected their joint concept for the record, subtitled as 'A Heart Play.'

Still, there was no doubt in my mind that 'Starting Over', 'Watching The Wheels', 'Woman', 'Clean Up Time', 'I'm Losing You', and 'Beautiful Boy' were all classic Lennon tracks, which would surely herald a triumphant return to the concert stage the following year if the rumours were true. Despite the album and single getting some rather cool reviews and lower-than-hoped-for chart placings, December 1980 began with the secure knowledge that John Lennon, now aged 40, was back on form after his five-year sabbatical, and ready to face his fans and the world once again. I was looking forward to the prospect of his and Yoko's likely return to the UK in the New Year, for promotion on radio, TV and in the press, as well as the possibility of meeting them once again, nearly 10 years after they'd left British shores.

But like millions of others on the planet, I recall only too well where I was upon hearing the tragedy unfolding in New York, late on Tuesday, December 8, or in London time the early hours of December 9. I was in bed at the flat I shared with my-then girlfriend, Elissia, in Parliament Hill, north London. As usual the radio alarm clock was tuned into Capital Radio and had switched itself on at eight o'clock. I awoke at that precise moment to hear the words,

"John Lennon, formerly of The Beatles..."

I didn't need to hear any more as I knew immediately what was coming; I just froze in the bed. I could not believe what I was hearing, this was the most crushing news imaginable. It was our generation's Kennedy moment, a totally senseless and deeply traumatic loss for music fans throughout the world, not to mention John's family and everyone who knew or had connections with him. John's unique personality, humour, music, lyrics, achievements and weird antics had been universally loved, respected or at least put up with for just 17 short years since The Beatles first found fame in 1963. But now some creepy, weird sicko had ended it all with a few shots from his loaded gun.

The irony was of course that John had been out of limelight for the last five of those 17 years, until just recently: bringing up son Sean, baking bread, sailing, travelling on his own and simply taking life at a relatively easy pace, as he fully deserved to do. I was feeling intensely angry and upset, as there hadn't been anything to match the scale of this assassination since JFK was shot, ironically in 1963.

I didn't quite know what to do that wretched morning, except to stay home, forget work and just watch TV as reports came in from various commentators in New York, Liverpool and London. Naturally many of John's solo records and Beatles songs were played non-stop on the radio, with special programmes planned for later in the day on all channels.

Eventually, I had to go out to meet Nigel and Mum at a pre-arranged 55th birthday lunch for her, at a small restaurant in Finchley. Inevitably it was a rather sombre affair, especially as the newsagent next door was already displaying a depressing fly-poster outside bearing the *Evening Standard*'s grim headline: "John Lennon Shot Dead".

It was hard not to talk about the tragedy, but Mum was also upset and deeply sympathetic to both Nigel and I, both recalling John in happier times.

Somewhat bizarrely, later that evening I was due to be playing drums in a medical student revue at University College Hospital, which had a full-size theatre within its premises. This was the second night of a two-week pre-Christmas run, with the show — entitled *The Enema Strikes Back* — consisting mainly of spoofs of popular TV shows, including *Dallas,* plus musical interludes. I was the replacement drummer for a 15-piece band which had rehearsed well for it, but only received the call a few days earlier from a panicked musical director, so had my work cut out.

The most-watched episode of *Dallas*, revealing 'Who Shot JR?', had been screened just two weeks earlier and was the biggest media story at the time. The show included a very funny skit on it, during which I had to recreate the moment of J.R. Ewing's infamous on-screen murder with three sharp beats on my snare drum, played in deathly silence.

As you can imagine, I was very much in two minds about taking part that night, but the show had to go on, so I performed wearing a hastily-made black armband. I'm sure that everyone in the audience must have been fully aware of what those three lonely drum beats also signified, as they reverberated around the theatre. Thankfully though, the otherwise highly entertaining revue did provide some form of light relief, as I played the rest of the show with an equally subdued band. However, my thoughts throughout most of the performance — and the whole run of the show —were of course focused on John Lennon.

Over the next few days, apart from playing drums in the show each evening, I was functioning pretty much on auto-pilot, still feeling extremely bitter that the unthinkable could have happened. I bought most of the papers to read and re-read the endless articles and tributes, written by people who knew John, and by many who didn't. They're all still stored in my archives, while quite a few of my friends made a point of calling to express their own sadness and sympathy.

One friend, Sandy Walker, told me later that at the time she was working for TWA in the same building that George Martin's AIR Studios was located in at Oxford Circus. She arrived at work during the morning of December 9, to find a horde of press outside waiting for Paul McCartney to arrive, which he did at virtually the same time as her. She ended up sharing the lift with a totally shattered Paul, who famously said he'd decided to go to work that day, as it was the only thing he could do to keep his mind off the tragedy. In the end he just spent many hours in the studio reminiscing about John with George Martin.

When his excellent third solo album, *Tug of War,* was eventually released, in April 1982, it included a highly poignant tribute to John, 'Here Today', a song which Paul includes in his shows to this day.

Meanwhile, Paul and Ringo featured on George Harrison's rather more upbeat tribute, 'All Those Years Ago', recorded in November 1980 and released as a single from his album *Somewhere in England* in May 1981. There were quite a few other notable tributes to John released over that period, most notably Elton John's 'Empty Garden (Hey Hey Johnny)'; Queen's 'Life Is Real (Song for Lennon)'; and Paul Simon's 'The Late Great Johnny Ace', along with offerings from many lesser-known artists, especially by some based in Liverpool.

I was also inspired to start writing my own tribute to John and The Beatles, which I made an extremely rough demo of at the time but didn't complete for many years. I eventually recorded 'Gold Songs' in 2009 with long-time producer and musician pal John Hamilton. The track features lead vocals by singer and actor Ben Champniss, who later played Shrimpy in BBC TV soap *EastEnders*. Also contributing were guitarist Dzal Martin, who plays a superb George-style solo on slide guitar; and Phil Nelson on backing vocals. You can read the lyrics at the end of this book, and also hear the track on the audiobook verion.

Life has never seemed quite the same since John was taken from us: the enormity of the crime, and the cruel timing of it, played on my mind for many months, if not years, after the event and still does today. It's shocking to realise that John innocently suffered the same fate as other celebrated pacifists, from Martin Luther King, Jr. to Mahatma Gandhi and Yitzhak Rabin.

Lennon's assassin is still imprisoned in New York State, having been turned down for parole 11 times in the past 20 years, the latest hearing in August 2020. Despite the conspiracy theories surrounding the case, he has never denied his crime, while still enjoying the luxury of life for the last 40 years. Unlike the late John Lennon, whose unique legacy of outstanding music and lyrics; artwork, books and poetry; and his endless wit and humour, along with his image and voice on records and on screen, will continue to live on, timelessly.

I rather wish that I'd made more of an effort to make contact with John in New York during the '70s, as he might well have responded. Who knows. At least I have my precious memories of meeting or seeing him on various occasions from 1965 through to 1971, as well as receiving that letter in 1969 which I stupidly lost.

Like Buddy Holly, Elvis Presley, Jimi Hendrix and others, John Lennon's extraordinary life and achievements are now encapsulated in a precisely definable time period, which has since spawned an infinite number of books, documentaries, record re-issues, conspiracy theories and speculation about 'what if'. John's unfairly shortened life has also inspired many good works, charitable projects and other notable endeavours in his name, and long may they continue.

And we all shine on...

Above left: With John's Aunt Mimi Smith in Sandbanks, Dorset, September 1981.

Above right: John's small bedroom, complete with gold discs above his single bed.

Left & below: The letter I received from Mimi after my visit.

Below: 'Harbour's Edge', the bungalow which John bought for her in 1965.

Left: Mimi was very happy that day, despite later writing *"it's been a bad time. Don't think I'll ever recover."*

Above left: Outside John and Mimi's old home 'Mendips' on Menlove Avenue in the '80s.

Above right: At the Adelphi Hotel in Liverpool for one of the annual Beatles conventions.

Left: With some of my Beatles books and scrapbooks, 1990s.

Below: At one of the Sotheby's music memorabilia auctions during the early '80s.

Left: The launch issue of SongLink, September 1993. *Below:* George Martin, Brian Matthew and Alan Freeman at the *Live at the BBC* launch, Abbey Road Studios 1996.

Above: George Martin with Neil Aspinall. *Left:* Derek Taylor, Jeff Lynne and Mark Lewisohn, at the *Beatles Anthology* launch.

Below left: Part of my 'Music for Montserrat' Slingerland kit.

Below right: Ringo with Zak Starkey and Joe Walsh at the Dorchester Hotel, April 1992.

Above left: Cynthia Lennon and Barbara Orbison at Abbey Road Studios, 2009.

Above right: Olivia Harrison and Judy Totton at the re-launch of George's *'I Me Mine'* book, Covent Garden 2017.

Below: Ken Scott, Chris Thomas, Sir George Martin and Glyn Johns, 2013.

Bottom left: With Harry Hill and Mike McCartney, 2013. *Bottom right:* With Rod Davis of the Quarrymen at Abbey Road Studios, 2009.

Top: My induction as a LIPA Companion in 2006, with Dr. Jörg Sennheiser, actress Lynda Bellingham, Sir Paul McCartney and Sir Ken Robinson.

Centre left: It's a double thumbs-up from Paul for the Stark brothers.

Centre right: LIPA Founding Principal Mark Featherstone-Witty OBE with Tony Moore.

Right: With Paul at LIPA Graduation Day, 2011.

Above left: With Sir George Martin at the Gold Badge Awards, 2011.

Above right: Sir George's final session at AIR Studios, with Keith Grant, Jason Hills and Francis Rockliff, 2000.

Left: With Bill Harry after we received our BASCA Gold Badge Awards, 1995.

Below: In Havana with fellow Beatles fans Glenn A. Baker, Mark Hudson and Ernesto Juan Castellanos, 1999.

Inset: Meeting President Fidel Castro, one of the highlights of my career.

Above left: The Blue Plaque for Brian Epstein at Sutherland House, June 2014.

Above right: Lining up for the unveiling: actor Andrew C. Lancel, Geoffrey Ellis, actress Vicki Michelle (Heritage Foundation chair) and DS.

Left: Actor Bill Nighy, Richard Porter, Mark Baxter, David Rosen and others with the 'Rooftop' Blue Plaque at 3 Savile Row, April 2019.

Below: Ringo and Paul onstage at the Odeon Leicester Square for the premiere of *Eight Days A Week* in 2016.

Above left: My original band Raw Deal in 1972 - Vince Lewis, DS, Dave Kent and Andy Leigh.

Above right: Playing with The Quarrymen in May 2013.

Left: Lining up for a press shot with Len Garry, John "Duff" Lowe, Rod Davis and Marko Laver.

Below: The Trembling Wilburys - DS, Dzal Martin, Andy McNish, Glen Knowler, Dave Collison, Marko Laver and Howard Robin.

CHAPTER 12

MOTHER SUPERIOR

In late summer, 1981, I drove down to Sandbanks, near Poole in Dorset, to meet the elderly lady who famously raised John Lennon from childhood, still living alone in the seaside home he'd bought for her in 1965. I'd never met his Aunt Mimi before, but arrived at her smart but modest bungalow with flowers in hand, after learning that a female acquaintance from the USA was staying with her.

Kathy Burns was a long-time Beatles fan from Minnesota, who visited and became good friends with Mimi in Liverpool during the 1960s. Nine months after John's murder, she returned on holiday to England to console Mimi in her ongoing grief at having lost her famous nephew in such shocking circumstances.

I didn't know quite what to expect when I rang the bell of the cosy-looking property, appropriately named Harbour's Edge, on Panorama Road, overlooking Poole Harbour. I knew the area slightly, having enjoyed a couple of family holidays during the '60s at the nearby Haven Hotel. However, Mimi immediately put me at ease with her extremely down-to-earth attitude and surprisingly wicked sense of humour, which became more evident during my time with her over the course of the weekend.

If Mimi was at all wary of having a male stranger from London in his late 20s spending a couple of days with her (but not sleeping there, as I'd booked a B&B), she never showed it. Instead, she offered me egg and chips with a cup of tea, which I quickly understood to be her way of showing that I'd passed the audition. During that first afternoon, she and Kathy chatted about all sorts of everyday things, Mimi mentioning to her at one point that she was in need of some kitchen utensils which had either been broken or had gone missing.

I made a mental note of this, and later went to the local shops to buy her a few pots and pans, plus some serving cutlery. She was extremely grateful for my small contributions to her rather basic domestic lifestyle, which must have been extremely difficult for her to cope with over the previous few months. Eventually, the three of us sat down in the lounge, which housed an elegant side-table upon which various mementos of John were placed. These included one of his Ivor Novello awards, plus framed photographs of his sons Julian and Sean. Meanwhile, above the door between the lounge and kitchen, was the legendary inscribed aluminium plaque which years before John had given to Mimi, quoting her own words when she paid £17 for his first-ever musical instrument:

"The guitar is all right as a hobby, John, but you'll never make a living at it."

I was quite in awe seeing so many items of priceless Lennon and Beatles memorabilia scattered around the house, as if it were the most natural thing in the world, which of course it was to Mimi. She started talking about John with a rather wistful but fiercely proud and protective voice, seeming rather pleased to have the opportunity to reminisce about him as a schoolboy; as the young tearaway turned Beatle; and as father to her two grand-nephews.

At one point, she opened a couple of drawers in a sideboard to show me John's old school tie from Quarry Bank High and other items from that period, along with an exercise book filled with all sorts of drawings and stories, much in the style of his brilliant 'Daily Howl' boyhood newspaper. Mimi had also preserved many of John's awards and gold discs, some hidden away but with a few on display in the small bedroom John used to stay in during occasional visits in the late '60s. Remarkably, Mimi always kept his single bed perfectly made up, and let me take a couple of photos of the room. It's true to say that her home contained an incredible treasure trove of Lennon artefacts and personal possessions, which Yoko later requisitioned from Mimi, and had transported to the Dakota building, where they presumably still are today.

Oh, Yoko ... not exactly Mimi's favourite subject, as it quickly became apparent, but she did demonstrate her sense of humour during one memorable moment in our conversation, which ran well into Saturday evening. At one point, the telephone rang and Mimi, thinking it might be Yoko calling from New York, put on a ridiculously frail 'little old lady' voice, saying,

"Hello, who is this?", before being satisfied that it wasn't Yoko at all, but a local friend.

She then quickly returned to her normal voice to continue with,

"Sorry, but I thought you might have been Yoko calling," which Kathy and I both found quite amusing.

Talking of Mimi's voice, she still retained a fair amount of her Liverpool accent and was well-spoken, but was certainly nothing like the over-posh character later portrayed by Kristin Scott Thomas in the 2009 film *Nowhere Boy*. I found Mimi to be great company, and was delighted to see her smiling and often laughing during our short time together.

As Kathy later said, Mimi seemed to come out of herself more in my presence, in a quite positive and possibly therapeutic way, just nine months after one of the most traumatic events of her life. She had also never forgotten that her younger sister Julia — John's mother — had also been violently killed, during a car accident in 1958. Mimi always considered this as being tantamount to murder by the off-duty policeman who had been driving the vehicle.

I found Mimi to be extremely open and forthright about John, Yoko, Cynthia and the other Beatles, as well as various others associated with the group. One question I particularly remember asking was whether John had ever come back to England to visit her in secret. He'd left the country in 1971, and despite travelling as far afield as Japan, Bermuda, Spain and even South Africa during the subsequent nine years, there were no reports of him ever coming back to visit his home country during all that time, which I always thought was somewhat curious.

John famously telephoned his Aunt Mimi at least once a week and also sent her letters and postcards on a regular basis, so why wouldn't he make the effort to see her if he was in travelling mode, especially knowing that she wasn't getting any younger? Could this be Yoko's influence, or concerns they may have had about his British passport and subsequent re-entry to the USA? I think it was probably the latter, as even though John eventually won his Green Card in 1976 after a five-year dispute with the FBI, his request for full residency status wouldn't have been granted until 1981.

However, Mimi's answer was simple and direct:

"Yes, he did come back to see me secretly, in disguise."

She was absolutely positive that this was the case, and quite adamant about it, although I couldn't pin her down on exactly when this mysterious undercover visit might have taken place. However, as it's never been proved or even mentioned by anyone else, including Yoko, I can only surmise that it was just wishful thinking on Mimi's part, which had engrained itself in her mind over the years. At the same time, I've often speculated how appropriate it would have been if it actually turned out to be true, and not just Mimi's most-likely lingering (double) fantasy.

The following day, I went with Kathy for a sight-seeing trip to nearby Brownsea Island, before returning to Harbour's Edge for tea. I eventually said my goodbyes to both her and Mimi, but not before we took some photos on the terrace behind the bungalow. Mimi looked especially relaxed and cheerful, posing with us and on her own with the harbour in the background. I'd like to think that my visit had done her some good that weekend. Sad to say, I didn't get to visit her again despite an open invitation, although I did keep in touch with her by phone on a few occasions. Not long after my visit she sent me an extremely nice letter in reply to mine, part of which is reproduced here:

Dear David,

It was nice of you to come and see me and to send the photographs, also thank you for your letter ... you did not impose in any way, in fact you were a help! I would have come with you & Kathy to Brownsea, but I was getting a bit tired ... Thank you for thinking about me, it has been a bad time. Don't think I'll ever recover. Glad you enjoyed your holiday, see you next time you are this way. Kind regards to your brother too.

All the best,
Mimi

I'd mentioned Nigel to her as, by sheer coincidence, our father had a sister named Mimi, who died of infection in the 1920s, aged just 13 years old. We only knew her from old family photographs, but had she survived we would have had our own Aunt Mimi, after whom Nigel's daughter is named. Incidentally, Mimi Brock-Stark was my guest at LIPA Graduation in 2018, where I took a very nice picture of her with Paul McCartney.

John's Aunt Mimi died at home on December 6, 1991, at the age of 85, the last survivor of five Stanley family sisters, despite being the eldest. According to an auxiliary nurse, Lynne Varcoe, who was present at her death, her last words were apparently,

"Hello, John."

Whereas, according to John's step-sister Julia Baird in her book, *Imagine This*, what she actually said was,

"I'm terrified of dying, I've been so wicked," which is slightly hard to imagine or to know exactly what she was referring to, so I'm keeping an open mind.

Mary Elizabeth 'Mimi' Smith was cremated at Poole Crematorium on December 12, 1991, followed by a wake at the local Harbour Heights Hotel, attended by Yoko, Sean and Cynthia, whom Mimi always had a soft spot for. Paul, George and Ringo all sent flowers, while Yoko apparently began to make arrangements to put Harbour's Edge up for sale the very same day. The bungalow was demolished in 1994 to make way for an ultra-modern four-bedroom, five-bathroom house, which was re-named 'Imagine' and recently valued at more than £7 million.

I'm just glad I managed to see the property as it originally was, and to meet its illustrious elderly occupant, who was nothing less than delightful. Although Mimi wasn't John's mother, I could clearly see a close family resemblance to him in both her facial features and personality. It seemed to me that Mimi possibly had as much influence on John as his mother Julia, perhaps even more so as his aunt survived her younger sister by more than 30 years. Plus, in a strange way, by meeting her I somehow felt that I'd also met my own Aunt Mimi, for a brief moment in time.

CHAPTER 13

GET BACK

During the early to mid-'80s, I was working for various music trade magazines, eventually becoming the editor of a monthly launched in 1984, *Sound Engineer & Producer*, which as the name suggests covered recording studios, pro-audio equipment and studio personnel. It brought me into contact with many well-known record producers and engineers, such as George Martin, Trevor Horn, Steve Levine, Robin Millar, Chris Kimsey, and John Leckie.

In late '84, we ran a major feature on Paul's new film project, *Give My Regards to Broad Street*, with the soundtrack album produced by George Martin and engineered by Geoff Emerick. If you've seen the film you'll know that it wasn't exactly Paul's finest hour, but our interview with George highlighted that he was extremely proud of the fact that all Paul's songs in the studio sequences were recorded totally live to picture.

Interviewer Richard Buskin and I both attended the film premiere, as did Paul and Linda. While the silly plot and script are best forgotten, the soundtrack included some impressive Martin arrangements of Beatles songs such as 'Eleanor Rigby' and 'For No One', as well as one of McCartney's finest solo songs, 'No More Lonely Nights', ending the film.

Incidentally, Richard often reminds me that, once the article was published, we went up to AIR Studios on Oxford Street to hand out extra copies of the magazine. We walked into the reception area to find Geoff Emerick and a few other engineers all sat on sofas during a break, avidly reading their copies.

A couple of years earlier, I met Paul and Linda at Abbey Road Studios when a reception was held to launch Brian Southall's 1982 book *Abbey Road: The Story of the World's Most Famous Recording Studios*, with a foreword written by Paul and a preface by George Martin. I may well have a unique copy, as I had it personally signed by Paul, Linda, George and Brian. I've also been fortunate to visit the studios on many occasions over the last 40-odd years for record launches, playbacks, songwriting weekends, and Beatles-related events.

Not a lot of people remember that between July 18 and September 11, 1983, Abbey Road was opened to the public for the first time, during renovation to parts of the studio. This was for a fascinating exhibition, *The Beatles at Abbey*

Road Studios (tickets £4.50, including refreshments), which also coincided with an auction of various items of vintage studio equipment.

The presentation included a guided tour hosted by studio manager Ken Townsend and others, with shows taking place three times a day. A reported 22,000 tickets were sold, with visitors being offered the opportunity to experience Studio 2 as the Beatles used it, with microphones and other equipment set up to replicate a typical recording session. Even Paul McCartney went along to one show, while George and Ringo also attended a private presentation.

Over recent years there have been a number of masterclasses held at the studios, hosted by Brian Kehew and Kevin Ryan, two American experts who wrote the superb 2006 book, *Recording The Beatles*. I've been to a couple of their sessions and they were indeed excellent, being enhanced by many Beatles tracks and out-takes played on high-quality audio or video clips, along with displays of much of the old equipment used to record them.

In November 1994, I was at the launch of *The Beatles at the BBC*, a double album of radio recordings premiered by Apple/EMI at Abbey Road with a reception and Q&A session. Producer George Martin, BBC producer and researcher Kevin Howlett, plus broadcasters Alan Freeman and Brian Matthew were all seated onstage to talk about the project. It was the first time that early recordings of the group performing on various BBC radio shows from 1963 to 1965 had been put together. The two mono albums compiled by George Martin for CD and vinyl included multiple tracks of studio dialogue, plus 56 songs, of which 30 had never been issued previously.

Exactly a year later, *The Beatles Anthology* was launched with another Apple/EMI reception at Abbey Road, featuring VIP guests George Martin, Neil Aspinall, Derek Taylor and Jeff Lynne, among others. This was a huge project, having been instigated back in the 1970s by Aspinall as a visual history of the group, under the working title, *The Long and Winding Road*. More than 20 years later, there was a massive promotional campaign for the six-part *Anthology* series on ITV, which started on November 26, 1995, along with a series of three double-CDs released at intervals, with superb artwork by Klaus Voormann, and two 'new' Beatles singles, 'Free As A Bird' and 'Real Love', restored from extremely rough Lennon cassette demos from the 1970s, co-produced with Jeff Lynne.

I thought that 'Free As A Bird' was very good, and was impressed by the clever way in which John's very basic recording had been enhanced and restructured. Paul and George both sang separately on the two middle-eight sections, complete with extra lyrics, while still keeping John's thinly-recorded voice at the forefront of each chorus. It may not have been one of his best songs, but the superb accompanying video certainly helped to improve its stature, making it a worthy addition to The Beatles' singles catalogue. I was only disappointed that, despite being given every promotional push, it didn't actually make No. 1, reaching only second place behind Michael Jackson's 'Earth Song'.

As for 'Real Love', released in March 1996, I would have rather that hadn't been released as a single at all, reaching only No. 4 in the UK and No. 11 in the USA, thereby somewhat degrading The Beatles' almost-impeccable chart record. Meanwhile, the *Anthology* launch was an excellent bash, during which I took a rather splendid shot of the late Derek Taylor, Jeff Lynne and Mark Lewisohn. At the time of writing, Mark is still working on *Turn On*, the second volume of his exhaustive Beatles trilogy, *All These Years*. Keep going Mark, we're all with you.

*

The mid-'80s also saw Paul's return to the concert stage after a six-year absence, with his closing performance of 'Let It Be' at *Live Aid* on July 13, 1985, during which his microphone notoriously cut out. I was in the stadium, feeling as frustrated as everyone else before normal service was eventually resumed as Bob Geldof, David Bowie, Alison Moyet and Pete Townshend jumped up to back Paul on the chorus, the entire ensemble then launching into the finale, 'Do They Know It's Christmas?'

It was an extremely long and hot day, but with many musical highlights, of which Queen's brilliant set is generally considered the best of the day. However, kudos must also go to Elvis Costello for delivering an inspired and quite unexpected acoustic version of 'All You Need Is Love'. He was the only artist to perform completely solo at Wembley Stadium that day, introducing The Beatles' anthemic 1967 single as an 'old English Northern folk song'.

Incidentally, I can also relate a little-known fact about the recording of Band Aid's record-breaking Christmas single, which kicked the whole thing off just eight months earlier. Apart from the *Daily Mirror*, which had exclusive media rights to the recording session, held on November 25, 1984, I was the only press person invited to Trevor Horn's SARM Studios in west London that Sunday, invited just two days earlier by engineer Stuart Bruce, who was working with Bob Geldof and Midge Ure on the record.

Somewhat embarrassingly, I had to decline Stuart's kind offer as I already had arrangements that Sunday, not having any idea how big the story was to become. Instead, I sent Richard Buskin in my place. Richard got straight through the heavy security at SARM's front door by mentioning me, with the rest of the press corps stuck outside, looking on incredulously as he walked in. In fact, he got extremely lucky and sneaked a few photos during the session, as well as being briefly seen in a Channel 4 documentary about it. But then he had been learning from the master.

*

Three months after *Live Aid*, I was invited to the taping of one of rock'n'roll's greatest TV spectaculars, filmed at Limehouse Studios in London's Docklands on October 21, 1985. *Blue Suede Shoes: A Rockabilly Session* featured Carl Perkins and friends, consisting of George Harrison, Ringo Starr, Eric Clapton, Slim Jim Phantom, Earl Slick, Roseanne Cash and Dave Edmunds, who also acted as musical director.

On arrival, I met my brother Nigel, who parked his Triumph motorcycle directly outside the studio entrance, subsequently seen in the opening sequence of the broadcast. Once inside, we had to go through security and be checked off the guest-list. Asked his name, Nigel — dressed in his usual leather jacket and jeans — simply replied 'Elvis' and was ushered straight through without question. Also there were Messrs. Buskin and Lewisohn, while the studio was full of fans and guests in eager anticipation of what proved to be a momentous evening.

It seemed slightly incongruous that filming was taking place in the relatively obscure (at that time) surroundings of London's Docklands, but it didn't matter a jot. The superb show featured a total of 18 rockabilly and rock'n'roll classics, while it was naturally George and Ringo we were most looking forward to seeing. This was George's first official performance in more than 10 years, and he was on top form, sharing vocals with Carl Perkins on 'Everybody's Trying To Be My Baby' and 'Your True Love', while Ringo sang 'Honey Don't' on his own and then 'Matchbox' with Carl and Eric.

The show inevitably concluded with a rousing version of Perkins' evergreen 'Blue Suede Shoes', before being repeated as the encore number, along with 'Gone Gone Gone'. It had all been well rehearsed, with very few retakes, while Carl was on great form and sporting what Richard always liked to call his 'poodle' wig. One notable absentee on the night was Paul McCartney, who also enjoyed a close musical relationship with Perkins over the years. I wonder if his inclusion on the bill was ever discussed. It would have certainly raised the show's legendary status to truly historic.

*

Paul was back at Wembley almost a year after *Live Aid* just as I was, but this time not in the Stadium but at the nearby Arena, for the Prince's Trust 10th anniversary *All-Star Rock Concert* on June 20, 1986. The superb line-up was one which almost matched *Live Aid*, including David Bowie duetting with Mick Jagger on 'Dancing in the Street', along with Elton John, Eric Clapton, George Michael, Mark Knopfler, Phil Collins, Rod Stewart, and others. Paul closed the show with 'I Saw Her Standing There', 'Long Tall Sally' and a grand finale of 'Get Back', with Tina Turner sharing vocals, most of the other stars joining in by the end.

A year later, in June 1987, it was George and Ringo's turn at Wembley Arena to get back on stage together, as headliners of another *Prince's Trust Rock Gala*. They closed the show with excellent versions of 'While My Guitar Gently Weeps', 'Here Comes the Sun' and 'With a Little Help From My Friends', supported by Eric Clapton, Phil Collins, Elton John, Dave Edmunds, and others.

It was especially good to see George on such great vocal and musical form and singing two of his classic Beatles numbers. Meanwhile, his and Ringo's presence inevitably led to rumours flying around the arena all evening that Paul would also be joining them on stage — but sadly not in our lifetime or theirs, apart from the three of them jamming a few times together at some extremely private functions. Firstly, at Eric Clapton and Pattie Boyd's wedding party in 1979; then again after Ringo's wedding to Barbara in 1981; and finally, during the filming of *The Beatles Anthology* in 1994, as well as recording the singles 'Free As A Bird' and 'Real Love'.

It would be more than two years before I next saw Paul on stage, during his massive 1989-90 *World Tour*. By that time, I was working in Amsterdam for Billboard magazine's European subsidiary, *Music & Media*, where I spent nearly two happy years as editor for the launch period of the company's European music industry directory. I've always enjoyed being involved in the international market since my Decca days, and the job and living in Amsterdam led to me making many more friends and colleagues around the continent.

In November 1989, I travelled with a few work colleagues to see Paul's show at the Ahoy Arena in Rotterdam, where we had backstage access afterwards, meeting up with promoter Barrie Marshall and wife Jenny, plus members of the band. Chris Whitten was the drummer on the tour, a superb player who also played on Paul's *Flowers in the Dirt* album, a highly underrated record in my view. It included Paul collaborating on four tracks with Elvis Costello, including the single 'My Brave Face', a song which I very much relate to Macca's late '80s period.

*

In late March 1992, George Harrison surprised everyone by announcing his first and only full-length British solo concert, to be held at the Royal Albert Hall on April 6. The show was held in aid of the Natural Law Party, a political group founded on the principles of transcendental meditation, whose affiliation with the Maharishi Mahesh Yogi had attracted George's support. The party was fielding a few candidates at the imminent General Election on April 9, and was attracting newspaper headlines, although more for the concept of 'flying yogis' than its political manifesto. George endorsed the party in a press release, stating:

"I want a total change and not just a choice between left and right. The system we have now is obsolete and not fulfilling the needs of the people. Times have changed and we need a new approach... the Natural Law Party is turning this election into a wonderful, national celebration and I am with them all the way."

The concert date also coincided with the press launch of Ringo's latest album, *Time Takes Time,* at the Dorchester Hotel that morning, to which I was invited. Ringo was also announcing his latest All-Starr Band summer tour, and turned up with son Zak Starkey and future brother-in-law Joe Walsh in tow (Joe married Barbara's sister Marjorie in 2008). I took a few shots of them, and also asked Ringo a question or two about the new album, which I later found to be rather good. What we didn't know, until later that evening, was that Joe would be guesting at George's show along with Gary Moore, while Ringo also took to the stage at the end to play on 'While My Guitar Gently Weeps' and 'Roll Over Beethoven'.

I was sitting in a loggia box close to the stage, along with Mark Lewisohn, Richard Buskin and others, while in the adjacent box were Carl Wilson and Mike Love of the Beach Boys, the latter having been at Rishikesh in India with The Beatles in 1968. It was great to see them next to us and exchange a few words, as I always tried to catch the Beach Boys in concert whenever they played in London.

I've also met Brian Wilson a few times, most memorably in 1985 for *Sound Engineer & Producer,* when Steve Levine was producing eponymous album *The Beach Boys* for CBS at Red Bus Studios, a mile or so away from Abbey Road. After we met in the control room, Brian invited me to join him in the studio for a unique one-to-one performance of his new song 'I'm So Lonely', played by him on a Fender Rhodes electric piano. I was sitting just a couple of feet away from him as he performed it, wondering if it was written about his former wife Marilyn, but also acutely aware that his brother Dennis had drowned just a few months earlier, during a terrible drinking and diving accident in Marina del Rey.

Brian was friendly enough, but I could tell he was much more focused on the new song than chatting with me at length. At the time, he was also very much under the influence of the notorious Dr. Eugene Landy, his psychotherapist, who was elsewhere in the studio. When the album was eventually released, 'I'm So Lonely' was fully embellished with synthesised brass, plus a real sax solo, but in my head I'll always hear Brian's plaintive voice singing it, all alone apart from me in the room that day.

Back at the Royal Albert Hall, George's benefit concert featured a great mix of solo and Beatles songs, including his surprise 1987 No. 1 comeback hit 'Got My Mind Set On You' from the *Cloud Nine* album, but sadly no Traveling Wilburys material. However, it was excellent to finally see and hear him play an entire show on his own, with a little help from son Dhani, Ringo, Joe Walsh, Gary Moore, Mike Campbell, Andy Fairweather Low, Ray Cooper, Chuck Leavell, Steve Ferrone, Greg Phillinganes, Will Lee, Katie Kissoon, and Tessa Niles.

George was on terrific form, having played a string of dates with Eric Clapton in Japan just four months earlier, although this show was strangely without Eric for some reason — perhaps medical. Otherwise the band was exactly the same, performing sublime renditions of 'Something', 'Here Comes the Sun', 'While My Guitar Gently Weeps' and many other Harrison classics. George looked extremely dashing in a white shirt and dark suit, also sporting a moustache and smiling a lot, despite appearing slightly nervous during parts of the show. However, by the end he must have felt pretty pleased that he'd pulled it off in front of an ecstatic home crowd after so many years, and in the company of so many gifted musical pals.

The concert was never officially released on video, but there are various bootleg versions available, as well as clips on YouTube. A totally triumphant and memorable evening, despite the Natural Law Party subsequently failing to win any seats at the General Election: no surprise there. Meanwhile, 10 years after his solo success that night, the Royal Albert Hall was to provide the perfect location for an equally memorable but much sadder occasion related to George, of which more anon.

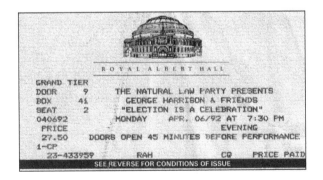

CHAPTER 14

I'VE BEEN WORKING LIKE A DOG

In September 1993 I launched *SongLink International*, a monthly trade magazine for music publishers and songwriters, which as well as providing regular interviews and industry articles also featured the all-important song leads. These confidential tips detailed which record labels, managers and producers were looking for new songs or album tracks for their artists or bands. The idea wasn't entirely new. I previously ran a similar publication on a smaller scale for another company before it went bust, but I greatly improved the concept and took most of the subscribers with me.

Luckily, I gained the support and respect of the industry right from the start, and over the past quarter of a century and more *SongLink* has helped place songs with the likes of Cliff Richard, Christina Aguilera, Tom Jones, Diana Ross, 'N Sync and many others all over the world, in all musical genres. Apart from the big British and American names, we've helped scores of indie artists as well as others on major labels who are big in their own countries but mostly unknown anywhere else.

Every music magazine needs a cover star, so the launch edition of *SongLink* featured Paul McCartney as boss of MPL Music Publishing, the largest division of MPL Communications. The company's general manager at the time was the late Alan Crowder, the subject of the very first *SongLink* interview, conducted by veteran music scribe Nigel Hunter, who wrote for *Disc* and other music papers during the '60s. Over the years, Nigel interviewed the great and the good of the music publishing and songwriting industries for *SongLink*, while MPL became regular subscribers in both their London and New York offices.

MPL Music is an extremely successful independent publishing company with a superb vintage catalogue, not only featuring Paul's own prolific output but also including many legendary songs by the likes of Buddy Holly, Fats Waller, Jelly Roll Morton, Louis Jordan, Bessie Smith, and Frank Loesser. These days the company's main focus is on getting song placements ('syncs') in film, TV and advertising, but it's also extremely strong on the musical theatre scores it owns, such as *Annie, Grease*, and *A Chorus Line*. The company also controls Paul's work on the forthcoming musical version of Frank Capra's classic 1946 film *It's A Wonderful Life,* which was due to open before Christmas 2020 but was delayed by Coronavirus. Paul has recorded versions of all the songs, with lyrics by him and Lee Hall (writer of *Billy Elliott* and *Rocketman*), so let's hope it eventually opens to big success.

Over the years, my work as *SongLink* publisher has taken me all around the world, connecting with a multitude of songwriters, artists, musicians and industry executives, many of whom became good friends or long-time colleagues. I've also been invited as a jury member to a number of international song contests, as far afield as Australia, Indonesia, Malta, Gibraltar, the Czech Republic, Ireland, Poland, Romania, and other exotic locations.

SongLink is used by many top professional songwriters as well as up-and-coming ones, and while it's become a lot harder to get 'cuts' with major artists these days, it's helped many subscribers score hits over the years. One anecdote still amuses me, when US songwriter Evan Pace started subscribing to *SongLink* during the '90s and received his very first issue by airmail. He wrote to me not long afterwards to say,

"Hey David, many thanks for SongLink and all the great leads. I sent one of my demos to Oleta Adams (of 'Get Here' fame) who's just recorded the song for her new album. I just wanted to say thanks and to ask you, does this happen every time?"

Not quite Evan, but your song pitch certainly did get lucky with Oleta, that album going on to be Grammy-nominated. A few years later, I got lucky myself in meeting the songwriter of 'Get Here', the wonderful Brenda Russell, at a major songwriting collaboration week in Havana, Cuba, under the name of 'Music Bridges Over Troubled Waters'. The event was the vision of Los Angeles songwriter Alan Roy Scott, with whom I was partners in the Unisong International Song Contest, which we launched the previous year. I accompanied our first Grand Prize winner — UK singer/songwriter Ruth Merry — to Havana, where she became quite a hit with all the big-name attendees.

These included an incredible array of American and British music legends, including Burt Bacharach, Bonnie Raitt, Joan Osborne, Gretchen Peters, Jimmy Buffet, Peter Buck of R.E.M., Stewart Copeland and Andy Summers of The Police, Peter Frampton, Mick Fleetwood, Don Was, and Lisa Loeb. On the Cuban side were such musical luminaries as Chucho Valdes, Alberto Tosca, Carlos Varella, Yosvany Terry and members of the bands Los Van Van, Sintesis and NG La Banda.

Music Bridges, held over a week in March 1999, was without doubt one of the highlights of my career, and a unique occasion in that special permission was given to American writers and artists to visit the island, under a cultural visa. The USA's blockade of Cuba since the revolution 40 years earlier had officially prevented US citizens from visiting since 1960.

The VIP visitors were co-writing every day with their Cuban counterparts in a suite of pop-up studios, installed in various rooms of the famous Hotel Nacional, to produce some inspiring and catchy songs. At the end of the week these were all played live in a special concert held at Havana's huge Karl Marx Theatre, a vast run-down old cinema. The concert was a huge success, the many singers and musicians joined on stage by actor Woody Harrelson, also there for the ride. He ended up dancing enthusiastically on stage to some of the superb performances, which went on till midnight.

The icing on the cake happened after the show finally ended, when our entire entourage — along with translator Ernesto Juan Castellanos and others — were escorted by two buses to President Fidel Castro's palatial headquarters in downtown Havana. The contrast between near poverty on the streets and Castro's huge modern building — with a succulent banquet spread out for us — was actually quite disconcerting. Castro was also present himself, meeting and greeting each of us personally, dressed in a smart business suit instead of his trademark military fatigues.

We all had to queue up patiently for our turn to meet him, with eagle-eyed armed guards watching over us. Ruth and I were sandwiched between Andy Summers in front and Mick Fleetwood behind, which rather reminded me of the old *Frost Report* sketch with Ronnie Corbett, Ronnie Barker and John Cleese with regards to our heights.

It was quite extraordinary, and somewhat surreal, to be shaking hands and speaking for a few minutes with Fidel Castro, albeit via a Spanish female interpreter. Apparently, he could speak good English but never did in public on principle. I invited him to London, as for some reason he'd never visited, but sadly he didn't take me up on my offer. He died in 2016, aged 90.

I was quite mesmerised by our brief encounter. He certainly had a huge aura of power and latent danger about him, his bodyguards' extremely visible weapons helping a great deal with that. A photograph and some video footage of us together was taken as I spoke with the great dictator, unique mementoes of a most remarkable final night in Havana.

I only wish I could have been back there the following year, on December 8, 2000, when Castro unveiled a memorial statue to John Lennon in Havana Park on the 20th anniversary of John's death, many years after The Beatles' music was officially banned on the island. Now a major sight-seeing attraction, the statue was given official state approval as Lennon was now considered — by a much more sympathetic regime — as an artist who had suffered, partly due to his campaigning against the Vietnam war, but also because he was aggressively pursued by the US government during the 1970s.

In 2002, Paul McCartney visited the island while on holiday in the Caribbean, but only to Santiago de Cuba, nearly 500 miles from Havana. Two years later, Sir George Martin was invited to the Cuban capital with the help of Ernesto Juan, as part of the 'Islands and Ideas' project, during which he conducted a concert of Beatles songs played by Cuba's National Symphony Orchestra at Havana's Amadeo Roldan Theatre. He also visited the John Lennon statue in the park and was photographed sitting next to it, a most poignant image.

It's also worth mentioning that the Rolling Stones played the biggest-ever free concert in Cuba in 2016, with an estimated audience of half a million people. Ernesto Juan was there too, with the Stones' superb *Havana Moon* film of the historic show being totally stunning.

However, the first major concert there by western artists took place as long ago as 1979, when the 'Havana Jam' saw Billy Joel, Stephen Stills, Kris Kristofferson, Rita Coolidge, Weather Report and others play as part of a three-day festival, co-sponsored by Columbia Records, local label Fania, and the Cuban Ministry of Culture. Ernesto, now based in Miami, has been working on a documentary film of the event for the past few years, which will hopefully be released sometime in the near future.

*

In October 1995, I was proud to be presented with a prestigious BASCA Gold Badge Award at the Savoy Hotel, just two years after launching *SongLink*. The annual awards are presented to individuals in the music, broadcast and related industries who have made significant contributions during their career in helping further the general awareness of British songwriters and composers.

Honourees at the salubrious lunchtime ceremony are usually advised well in advance that they're on the list, so they can arrange for family and friends to share the special day with them. But no, not me. I was attending the star-studded event as a guest of the Academy on my own, when, right at the end of the awards presentation, BASCA chairman and host Guy Fletcher suddenly started talking about someone in the room ...

"Who's been providing an important service for songwriters for the last few years," before announcing me as an extra last-minute Gold Badge recipient.

Talk about being caught on the hop: I jumped up on stage to make a ramshackle speech off the top of my head, while many in the room smiled and applauded at my predicament. A lovely gesture by BASCA, but it would have been nice to have had some of my family there to share it with me, especially my parents. However, it was a great honour, especially as I was the youngest person to receive a Gold Badge up to then, at just 42.

My fellow recipients on the day included Beatles author Bill Harry, Barbara Dickson, Madeline Bell, Larry Adler, Rolf Harris, Dennis Lotis, musicologist Pete Frame, songwriter Geoff Stephens, The Barron Knights, and the Ted Heath Band. I've attended most of the ceremonies over the years and have also helped a few select friends receive their own badges (actually miniature gold tuning forks), and it's always been an extremely special day in the music industry calendar.

One memorable Gold Badge lunch with a particular Liverpool flavour took place in 2008, when Sir Ken Dodd and my pal, writer/broadcaster Spencer Leigh of BBC Merseyside, were both honoured for their outstanding contributions to music. To coin a phrase, I was extremely tickled indeed to meet and chat with 'Doddy', whom I quickly discovered to be one of the nicest, most genuine people in showbusiness. A true legend of comedy, and also the singer who beat The Beatles in the charts to achieve the biggest-selling British single of 1966 with 'Tears'.

*

Another landmark award in my career took place at Liverpool's Philharmonic Hall in July 2006, when I was inducted as a 'Companion of LIPA' by Sir Paul McCartney and Mark Featherstone-Witty O.B.E., the founding principal and CEO of the Liverpool Institute for Performing Arts. LIPA was formally opened by Her Majesty The Queen in 1996, after seven years of planning and fundraising by Mark, with invaluable help from Paul as lead patron, as well as Sir George Martin, who was also integral to its early development.

This outstanding centre of excellence for students of music, recording, theatre and dance — both as performers and also as management, technology and production trainees — is based in Paul's old school, the Liverpool Institute (also attended by George Harrison), now fully modernised into one of the finest facilities of its kind in the world. I was aware of the plans for LIPA right from the start, when old bricks from the original Cavern Club were sold off to kick-start fundraising for the ambitious project in the late '80s. Eventually £20 million was found, before the official opening on June 7, 1996.

My professional involvement with LIPA started in the early 2000s, when I was invited to present a masterclass to students about *SongLink*, my career, and how new songwriters can make headway along the rocky road of the music business. I've done this many times over the years, as well as arranging other guest speakers to visit, such as songwriter Guy Chambers, known for his work with Robbie Williams and others, and film composer David Arnold, of *James Bond* movie fame.

The weekly master-classes usually take place in the Paul McCartney Auditorium, an intimate theatre space which has hosted many illustrious speakers in recent years, such as Nile Rodgers, Don Black, Dame Judi Dench, Mark Ronson, Joan Armatrading, John Hurt, Robin Gibb, Arlene Phillips, Trevor Horn, and Billy Ocean.

To be included in such exalted company as a Companion is a real honour, limited to a few people each year who have all made positive contributions to

LIPA. This is normally in the form of donating time and expertise to host master-classes or being interviewed on stage by Mark about their illustrious careers.

A year or two before my induction, I realised there was no special award given to songwriter students on Graduation Day, unlike for students of recording, theatre and dance. I therefore offered to instigate the annual 'SongLink Prizes', which I've presented each year since, awarding two songwriter students with cheques, certificates and career advice based on the quality of their music, lyrics, originality and commercial appeal. The musical standard at LIPA is always incredibly high, and while it's often hard to choose two winners out of so many good submissions, the cream usually rises to the top.

On Graduation Day 2006, my fellow Companions to be inducted consisted of the actress Lynda Bellingham; motivational speaker Sir Ken Robinson; electronics pioneer Dr. Jörg Sennheiser; and actor Terence Stamp, honoured in his unavoidable absence.

The format is virtually the same each year, with the new Companions and other VIP guests all gathering in the Philharmonic Hall's Green Room ahead of the ceremony, to be greeted by Mark Featherstone-Witty. The first big moment occurs when Paul arrives, often returning to Liverpool especially for the occasion while in the middle of a big summer tour. It's always a privilege to meet him there, and he always makes sure to greet old friends and LIPA staffers, and having his picture taken with all the new Companions for the traditional pre-ceremony photograph.

A procession eventually starts lining up in the room, with Paul and Mark leading two columns of guests into the packed hall, to riotous applause from the students and their families. We all take our seats ready for the ceremony to begin, usually preceded by a short celebratory film focussing on student achievements over the past academic year. During the next three hours, more than 200 students receive Graduation certificates from Paul, while Mark introduces each new Companion at regular intervals, upon which they are required to make a speech.

By sod's law, I had to follow one of Britain's most celebrated orators, Sir Ken Robinson (who sadly passed away in August 2020), who made such a brilliant, inspiring and humorous speech that I thought I may as well pack up and go home. Somehow, I got through mine unscathed, with references to how The Beatles and Paul had influenced my life and music industry career, as well as talking about my achievements. I finished with a few traditional words of encouragement to all the graduates, basically along the lines of,

"Follow your instincts in choosing your goals. If I can do it, so can you."

I must have made some impact on Paul, as during the reception afterwards he said to me,

"I didn't know you'd done all that."

On other occasions we might discuss the latest SongLink Prize winners and nominees, while he's usually happy to talk about his recent activities as well. For one day each year, Paul also makes a point of spending time with each songwriter student at LIPA. These usually take place during the Easter term, with Paul conducting short one-to-one sessions, during which he's even been known to start co-writing new songs with some of the students. Now that's what I call integrity and dedication, otherwise known as being a 'mensch'.

Paul's brother, Mike McCartney, was also present during my induction, along with Neil Aspinall, the head of Apple Corps and long-time Beatles confidant, who sadly died a couple of years later. Mike is a LIPA Graduation regular, often with wife Rowena, while other guests over the years I've been attending have included Sir George Martin and son Giles, Midge Ure, Trevor Horn, Mike Batt, Tom Robinson, Janice Long, Noddy Holder, John Hurt, Nitin Sawhney, Hugh Padgham, Kevin Godley, Tony Platt, Nikolas Grace, Rowena Morgan, Seymour Stein, and Woody Harrelson.

I'm delighted to have helped many talented young songwriters at the start of their careers, such as Juan Zelada, Lauren Flynn, Edwin Pope, Evelyn Burke, Joe Kenny, Cameron Warren, and Ian Janco. For a few years, I also organised an annual 'LIPA Night' at a top London music venue, The Bedford in Balham, in conjunction with MC extraordinaire Tony Moore. Tony is also a brilliant singer/songwriter, and a great friend, over the years helping the likes of Ed Sheeran, Paolo Nutini and KT Tunstall, among many others.

A coach-load of songwriter students from LIPA used to trek down the motorway from Liverpool to perform at the award-winning venue, while we'd also receive a special message of congratulations from Paul which I'd read out onstage. As Tony often says,

"LIPA students just seem to have that 'extra something' or 'the X-Factor' to make them stand out from the crowd," which still very much applies today.

LIPA has become an exceptionally important institution in my career, and one with which I've been extremely proud to have been closely associated for the last two decades. Big thanks to Mark Featherstone-Witty, Martin Isherwood, Ged McKenna, Keith Mullen, Kathy Cross, Eddie Lundon, and everyone else I've dealt with there over the years. You're all very special people.

CHAPTER 15

A LITTLE LIKE A MILITARY MAN

I was most fortunate to meet Sir George Martin on many occasions over the years, and remember him fondly as the kindly, modest gentleman he always was, whether in public or private. Our paths often crossed at industry awards, record launches, receptions and other events, where he always had time for a few words, usually with a smile and self-effacing comment — especially if anyone praised his work or integral role in helping to shape British music.

However, he really was the father figure of the British recording industry, being rightfully honoured by virtually every major music body for his outstanding contributions, notably PRS for Music; BASCA; the BPI; and APRS, the Association of Professional Recording Services, of which he was Life President. Plus, of course, he was knighted by Her Majesty The Queen at Buckingham Palace in 1996, an honour he fully deserved. It's hard to imagine The Beatles' recordings without his enormous input, especially in the group's later career and particularly on *Abbey Road*. He played a massive role as part of their musical chemistry as an unseen collaborator, providing essential order, perfect arrangements and structure to their incredible songwriting abilities.

As mentioned earlier, I first saw George at the age of 15 when I snapped him walking into EMI Studios in the spring of '66. I subsequently met him many times in later years at Abbey Road, when he would invariably be in attendance for any Beatles-related events, such as the launches of Brian Southall's book on the studios in 1982; *The Beatles at the BBC* and *Anthology* launches, and many others.

George also wrote a number of excellent books himself, about his work and career, some of which were launched at the studios, along with various TV programmes he was involved with. In October 1988, he was the recipient of the seventh 'British Music Industry Trusts' Award', with a dinner held at Grosvenor House Hotel that I attended, while during the '90s and early 2000s I seemed to bump into him and his wife Lady Judy almost every few weeks at some event or other.

When AIR Studios moved in 1991 from Oxford Circus to Lyndhurst Road in Hampstead, very close to where I live, George gave a private tour of the superb facility — located in a former huge Victorian church — to myself and Ernesto

Juan, who was over from Cuba on a rare visit. George was more than happy to give us an hour or more of his time, as well as recalling a few of his many studio anecdotes along the way.

I'm reminded of one of those (non-Beatles) stories by Mo Foster, session bassist extraordinaire for many top artists back in the day. These included Jeff Beck on his *Blow by Blow* album, which was produced by George at the original AIR Studios in Oxford Street, as Mo recalls in his excellent book, *British Rock Guitar*:

"Jeff was fastidious about over-dubs but never seemed to be happy with his solos. A few days after a recording when he'd had time to digest his own performance, he would telephone George and say, 'I think I could do a better one on this track' and they would return to AIR to try again. Jeff would play over and over until he was satisfied that he had performed his best. A couple of months went by and George received another phone call from Jeff saying, 'I want to do this solo again.' Bemused, George replied 'I'm sorry Jeff but the record's in the shops!'"

One enjoyable event at AIR (Associated Independent Recording) was the 1994 launch of *The Glory of Gershwin,* a special tribute album produced by George. The album was recorded to celebrate the 80th birthday of George and Ira Gershwin's lifelong friend, the American harmonica virtuoso Larry Adler, who happened to live just down the road from the studios and myself.

Adler played on the album with such guest vocalists as Kate Bush, Peter Gabriel, Elton John, and Cher, with one of the highlights being Kate's version of 'The Man I Love', complete with a masterful arrangement by George. The launch party was a glittering occasion, with the studios decked out in tasteful vintage style, VIP guests also including Ringo Starr and wife Barbara among others.

Three years later, in September 1997, AIR Lyndhurst was used as the rehearsal space for Sir George's *Music for Montserrat* concert, held at the Royal Albert Hall the following evening. Top musicians came together to raise funds for the picturesque Caribbean island, where George had established AIR Montserrat Studios in the mid-'70s. However, the island had been doubly hit by a huge hurricane in 1989, followed by a series of eruptions by the Soufrière Hills volcano within the space of 10 years.

Another major eruption in June 1989 subsequently left the southern half of the island completely devastated, including AIR Studios as well as the capital Plymouth, causing mass evacuations from the uninhabitable region. With Sir George's concern and action, the proceeds from the Albert Hall show, plus a special Sotheby's auction; DVD/CD sets; merchandising sales; and donations would be used for immediate relief, as well as helping to fund the building of a new cultural centre, eventually gifted to the islanders in 2006.

The concert was arranged and produced by Sir George himself, and starred Paul McCartney, Elton John, Eric Clapton, Phil Collins, Mark Knopfler, Sting, Carl Perkins, Midge Ure, Jimmy Buffett, and others, all of whom recorded at AIR Montserrat at one time or another. I got to hear about the rehearsals and walked round to AIR to see what was going on, bumping into Midge Ure in the café for a quick cuppa as entrance to the actual rehearsal was extremely restricted.

However, my eyes were diverted by some large half-opened cardboard boxes sitting in the reception area. These turned out to contain a unique set of drums, especially custom-made for the show and shipped over for the occasion from the USA. The kit was built by Slingerland, a legendary percussion brand more usually associated with Buddy Rich, Gene Krupa and other jazz greats, rather than rock players.

But now the drum firm was owned by the Gibson company of Nashville, which was also providing a bunch of custom guitars for the show, along with artist relations manager Pat Foley, who flew over for the week. The drums had all been air-brushed in Montserrat colours of pale blue, orange and green, a beautiful kit which would stand out at the following evening's performance, as played by top session drummer Ian Thomas.

The show itself was a total triumph, the Albert Hall's nearest equivalent to a mini-*Live Aid*. In fact, it featured many stars who also played the 1985 charity event at Wembley Stadium, brought together again to do their bit for Sir George's equally worthy cause.

Phil Collins opened proceedings with 'Take Me Home', while stand-out moments included Mark Knopfler, Sting and Eric Clapton performing 'Money For Nothing'; Clapton's 'Layla' with Knopfler; Sting's 'Message In A Bottle'; Elton's 'Your Song' and 'Don't Let The Sun Go Down On Me'; Carl Perkins' 'Blue Suede Shoes' — his last major performance as he died four months later, aged just 65; Jimmy Buffett's 'Volcano'; and legendary Montserratian musician and songwriter Arrow (real name Alphonsus Celestine Edmund Cassell, MBE), performing his worldwide Soca dance hit, 'Hot Hot Hot'.

Inevitably, the finale set was provided by Paul McCartney, who performed 'Yesterday', 'Hey Jude' and 'Kansas City', plus a great version of *Abbey Road*'s side two medley along with Clapton, Elton, Collins and Knopfler, with Sir George conducting.

It was a totally magical night, which helped raise desperately-needed funds for the tiny population of disaster-stricken Montserrat, but there was more to come. The following evening, a specially-arranged Sotheby's auction was held at the Hard Rock Café by Hyde Park Corner, hosted by Sir George, with the express intent of selling some of the instruments played at the concert to the highest bidders.

I naturally went along and was rather surprised to see that superb Slingerland drum kit spread out on the floor in a somewhat piece-meal fashion, not being set up properly at all. Most of the attention was being focused on the main auction item, a Gibson Les Paul signed by all the show's stars, including Paul, which went for £15,000 — a reasonable amount in those days, but worth a lot more now. Sir George was standing at the auction block along with auctioneer Jon Baddeley and expressed his pleasure at the result.

Next up were the drums, which started at a ridiculously low bid of £500 before slowly creeping up past the £1,000-mark. I was quite taken aback, as apart from being so immaculately custom-painted for the concert, it was actually worth a lot more as a new kit in its own right. However, on realising that it didn't seem to have anywhere near as much interest as the guitar, I raised my hand as the bids slowly increased until I was the only person left in the bidding.

Amazingly, the kit was suddenly mine, and at a price I could actually afford: I was extremely surprised, but naturally as pleased as punch. Even though Sir George was probably a tad peeved that it didn't raise anything like as much as the guitar, he was gracious enough to congratulate me on my purchase. The deal was made even sweeter when I mentioned to auctioneer Jon Baddeley — who I knew from previous auctions — that I had my car outside, cheekily asking him whether it would be possible to take the kit home that same night and pay Sotheby's the next day.

Quite surprisingly he agreed, and to this day it remains one of my most prized possessions. I've played it a few times on stage, but it's now become more a part of my home furniture and a reminder of an incredible night.

*

In early 2001 I received a call from Oxford-based film, TV and stage composer Francis Rockliff, a subscriber to *SongLink* at the time. He said he was just around the corner from me at AIR Lyndhurst, working with Sir George Martin on a special project. He asked if I could get over there with a camera as quickly as possible, as George had just announced that it was to be his last-ever recording session.

A few minutes later, I walked into the control room at AIR's Studio One. George was sat at the mixing console with Francis and top recording engineer Keith Grant, who worked with The Beatles, the Stones, The Who, Led Zeppelin, Jimi Hendrix, and many others. For years Keith was based at Olympic Studios in Barnes, a highly popular and inspirational character who sadly went to the studio in the sky in 2012.

Francis explained that Sir George had composed and produced a six-minute soundtrack for a forthcoming online conference, *Aviation 2001*, which would also be played during an RAF fly-past in Oxfordshire later that year. Entitled

The Stringbag Serenade, the piece was performed by the London Chamber Orchestra and commemorated the Swordfish bi-planes that a young George Martin flew during World War II during his time with the Royal Navy's Fleet Air Arm.

Sir George expanded on this at the time by writing,

"The music is a medley of tunes which the pilots and crew used to sing, to keep their spirits up when they were flying in what could be very tricky conditions. The Swordfish was an extraordinary aircraft, and was nicknamed the Stringbag by the men who worked with them. I now work alongside the Swordfish Heritage Trust, helping to raise the profile of historic aircraft, and also raise money to keep them in the skies."

The piece had already been recorded, while George and Keith were in the very final stages of mixing it. In fact, they had been waiting for me to arrive before playing it through one last time on the studio monitors. It proved to be a highly atmospheric and uplifting piece, reminding me that George was not only a brilliant producer, but also a highly-respected composer who had written incidental music for all The Beatles' films, as well as scores for *Live And Let Die* and *The Family Way*. He also penned BBC Radio One's memorable 'Theme One', the very first piece of music heard on the station in September 1967.

Some 34 years on, having only come out of semi-retirement in the mid-'90s to work on *The Beatles Anthology* project, George pressed 'stop' at the end of the *Stringbag* playback and casually announced to us,

"That's me done, then."

It was a rather surreal moment to take in, but moments later George, Keith, Francis and Jason Hills (of sponsors RMC plc) assembled for a group photo which I took at the mixing desk, with a model Stringbag plane placed in front of them. And that was almost that for Sir George, until he was persuaded to come out of retirement once again in 2006, to work with son Giles on re-mixing 80 minutes of Beatles music for *Love*, the spectacular *Cirque du Soleil* show in Las Vegas, which also resulted in a top-three soundtrack album.

Stringbag Serenade and *Love* were therefore the closing chapters in George's illustrious career. The previous 60 years or more had seen him not only working with The Beatles but many other artists, including Cilla Black, Gerry & the Pacemakers, Billy J. Kramer, The Fourmost, Jeff Beck, John McLoughlin, America, Kenny Rogers, Jimmy Webb, Neil Sedaka, UFO, Cheap Trick, Gary Brooker, Bernard Cribbins, Peter Sellers, Spike Milligan, Elton John, Ringo Starr, his own George Martin Orchestra, and of course Paul McCartney.

Meanwhile, the highlight of the (now sadly-defunct) APRS year was the annual 'Sound Fellowship Lunch', which took place at Kensington Roof Gardens every November, with Sir George and Lady Judy attending as guests of honour whenever possible.

At the 2013 lunch, I took another memorable photograph, of Sir George with three old colleagues also involved with the production or engineering of Beatles records, namely Ken Scott, Glyn Johns and Chris Thomas. It was a great shame that George's former sidekick Geoff Emerick wasn't also there that day, as he died a couple of years later. In addition, former Abbey Road manager Ken Townsend (the man who invented the 'flanger') and technical engineer Dave Harries were always present as APRS stalwarts.

Another special moment took place in Liverpool some years ago, when I walked into a near-empty pre-reception during my early arrival at LIPA Graduation Day, to find Paul McCartney standing in deep conversation with Sir George, a guest at that year's event. I thought I'd better just walk past without bothering them, but as I did, Paul suddenly swung round to exclaim,

"Alright, Dave?" while George merely smiled and said,

"Hello, nice to see you again." Always the gentleman.

*

Sir George Martin, CBE died on March 8, 2016 at his home in Wiltshire, at the age of 90. He is survived by his wife of nearly 50 years, Lady Judy Martin, and his four children from two marriages: Giles, Lucie, Alexis and Greg. Sadly, I was unable to attend his memorial service at St. Martin's-in-the-Fields two months later, which was attended by Paul, Yoko, Elton John and many others, including James Bay, who sang 'While My Guitar Gently Weeps'.

I'll leave the last words on Sir George to Paul, speaking at the service:

"I have so many wonderful memories of this great man that will be with me forever. He was a true gentleman and like a second father to me. He guided the career of The Beatles with such skill and good humour that he became a true friend to me and my family. If anyone earned the title of the fifth Beatle it was George. From the day that he gave The Beatles our first recording contract, to the last time I saw him, he was the most generous, intelligent and musical person I've ever had the pleasure to know. My family and I, to whom he was a dear friend, will miss him greatly and send our love to his wife Judy and their kids Giles and Lucie, and the grandkids. The world has lost a truly great man who left an indelible mark on my soul and the history of British music."

CHAPTER 16

THE ACT YOU'VE KNOWN FOR
ALL THESE YEARS

Sadly, the other George (Harrison) died from lung cancer on November 29, 2001, not such a surprise as his illness had been widely reported for some time, but nevertheless a huge shock and major media story when it happened. Two Beatles gone in a little under 21 years: just tragic. Like John, George was cremated in the city in which he died — in his case Los Angeles — while his ashes were later scattered by his wife Olivia and son Dhani at the Ganges and Yamuna rivers in India.

I felt extremely fortunate to have met George a few times, getting to know first-hand what a friendly and quite unassuming fellow he was. And with a great sense of humour, as his self-effacing cameo appearances on The Rutles' *All You Need Is Cash*, *Rutland Weekend TV*, and *Saturday Night Live* all demonstrated. He had been working on his final album, *Brainwashed,* eventually released in November 2002 and containing some excellent tracks.

These included the Grammy-nominated opener 'Any Road', along with the instrumental 'Marwa Blues', which won a Grammy Award for Best Pop Instrumental. The closing title-track also demonstrated that George never lost his sense of injustice or humour about his ongoing problems with the modern world.

Exactly one year after his passing, I was back at the Royal Albert Hall for the *Concert for George*, a huge celebration of his life organised by Olivia. The atmosphere in the iconic venue was highly reverential, with flowers decked all around, a poignant mid-'60s photo of Beatle George with his Gretsch guitar hanging over the stage. I was invited by Joe Brown's long-time PR lady Judy Totton and manager John Taylor, both good friends, to sit in Joe's box, perfectly positioned directly opposite the stage — in fact, just overlooking the seats Mum and I had occupied when we'd met George there back in 1974.

If you've never seen the concert on TV, DVD or online, I suggest you do, as it was a truly magical occasion. Opening with a traditional prayer and dedication, entitled 'Sarveshaam' by Ravi Shankar, this was followed by his daughter, Anoushka, playing sitar on 'Your Eyes', before joining Jeff Lynne, Dhani Harrison and others for an acoustic version of 'The Inner Light'. A 20-minute orchestral version of Ravi's 'Arpan' followed, conducted by Michael Kamen, a supremely-gifted composer in his own right, who sadly died just under a year later.

The outstanding line-up included most of George's closest musical friends and collaborators, including — deep breath — Paul and Ringo, Billy Preston, Eric Clapton, Klaus Voormann, Gary Brooker of Procol Harum, Andy Fairweather Low, drummer Jim Capaldi from Traffic, Joe Brown, Tom Petty, Jim Keltner, Jim Horn, Albert Lee, Jools Holland, Chris Stainton, Henry Spinetti, Ray Cooper, Tom Scott, and backing vocalists Katie Kissoon, Tessa Niles and Sam Brown.

There were also four members of Monty Python's Flying Circus present: Eric Idle, Terry Gilliam, Terry Jones and Michael Palin, along with Neil Innes, Carol Cleveland and special guest Tom Hanks, all delivering hilarious versions of Python classics 'Sit On My Face' and 'The Lumberjack Song'. Just superb.

George's spirit was undoubtedly felt by everyone in the audience that evening, while all the performers excelled with their versions of George's songs. Stand-out moments included Tom Petty's versions of 'Taxman', 'I Need You' and 'Handle With Care', with Jeff Lynne joining him on the latter, while Eric Clapton shared lead vocals with Paul McCartney on 'While My Guitar Gently Weeps'. Paul also sang 'For You Blue' and 'Something' before going into an initially mournful, but ultimately joyous version of 'All Things Must Pass', while Ringo performed 'Photograph', the hit he co-wrote with George, as well as singing Carl Perkins' classic 'Honey Don't' once again.

However, it was Billy Preston's rapturous version of 'My Sweet Lord' which stole the show for me, a truly inspirational performance on which he was joined by Paul, Ringo and Eric, with Klaus Voormann on bass, Mike Mann on slide guitar, and Dhani Harrison on backing vocals. Following a final version of 'Wah Wah' with virtually everyone on stage, the concert concluded with Joe Brown's solo performance of 'I'll See You in My Dreams', the old standard written in 1924 by Gus Kahn and Isham Jones. It proved to be one of the most touching moments of the night, and the one which many people who were there still talk about today.

I felt privileged to be sat in Joe's box, having met and seen him play live on many other occasions, including his 65th birthday party at home in Henley-on-Thames in 2006. George had been best man at Joe's second wedding to the lovely Manon, while scattered around their house were a few discrete mementoes to his late Beatle pal, including a ukulele George had given to Joe, in pride of place on his piano.

Joe always pays musical tributes to his late mate during his shows, playing at least one of George's songs, including the occasional Traveling Wilburys number, and still ends each concert with 'I'll See You in My Dreams'. One of the great British rock survivors from the 1950s, Joe Brown is a superb musician on virtually any stringed instrument and an extremely likeable chap, now in his 80th year. And still with a full head of that amazing spiky blonde hair.

*

Paul and Ringo have both continued to tour extensively, Paul with his excellent four-piece band (Paul 'Wix' Wickens, Rusty Anderson, Brian Ray, and Abe Laboriel Jr.); and Ringo with his ever-changing All-Starr Band (although it seems to have settled down to the same line-up in the past few years, including Colin Hay, Hamish Stuart, Gregg Bissonette, Steve Lukather, Gregg Rolie, and Warren Ham).

While I've seen Paul in concert many times over the years, Ringo's band has only played a handful of shows in the UK. I first saw them on his 52nd birthday, July 7, 1992, when he had a terrific line-up featuring Dave Edmunds, Joe Walsh, Todd Rundgren, Timothy B. Schmidt, Burton Cummings, and Tim Cappello; while I also saw the band during the '90s at Radio City Music Hall in New York.

A few good pals have toured with Ringo over the past 20 years, including Randy Bachman (Bachman Turner Overdrive and the Guess Who), Paul Carrack, and 10cc's Graham Gouldman. They've all told me how they cherished being invited by Ringo, with the opportunity of playing Beatles and solo songs with him, as well as one or two of their own. Although Ringo's 2020 tour was cancelled because of Coronavirus, he's hoping to be back on the road in 2021, by which time the eldest Beatle will be going on 81.

*

A few others of the many shows I've seen by Paul McCartney stick out in the memory, including the *Back in the World Tour* at King's Dock in Liverpool in June 2003, where I also had a pass for a private after-show party for Paul's family and friends. Macca was on a real high that night, ending up jamming on a small stage with his cousin Ron, who was spinning Elvis records over the PA. I remember Paul excitedly changing the words to 'Blue Suede Shoes' to some rather rude lyrics about a chicken (or veggie) vindaloo, hysterically funny at the time.

By complete contrast, in 1991 I was at the first London performance of Paul's *Liverpool Oratorio,* performed at the Royal Festival Hall by the Royal Liverpool Philharmonic Concert Orchestra with Dame Kiri Te Kanawa, Sally Burgess and Willard White, and conducted by Carl Davis. The concert was extremely moving as the story follows Paul's own lifeline, with the main character being Shanty, born in 1942 in Liverpool and raised to believe that where you are born carries certain responsibilities with it.

Six years later, I attended the world premiere of *Standing Stone,* the instrumental version of a long poem Paul had written in reflection of how a Celtic man might have wondered about the origins of life and the mysteries of the universe.

Paul has many other strings to his bow, including poetry, painting, caricatures and children's books, but the one thing I would dearly love to see is a stage musical incorporating all his '20s and '30s-style songs, such as 'When I'm 64', 'Honey Pie', 'You Gave Me the Answer', 'Walking In The Park with Eloise' and others. The kind of show that his Dad, Jim McCartney would have been extremely proud of, maybe even based on his time running Jim Mac's Jazz Band.

*

In May 2004, I was invited to the final rehearsal of Paul's *Summer Tour* at what was still named the Millennium Dome, before it was transformed into the incredibly successful O2 Arena that it is today. The North Greenwich venue took the industry crown as the busiest in the world during 2018, and is one I've been to many times since it opened, having seen Paul, the Stones, The Who, Queen, Fleetwood Mac, Neil Young, and Led Zeppelin's legendary comeback show there, among many others.

I arrived alone in the early afternoon as instructed, fully expecting to see a queue of locals and other fans waiting outside to be admitted for a special Macca tour preview. But no, not a soul in sight. I passed through security and entered the cavernous tent, as this was before any of the many O2 attractions, restaurants and bars had been built inside. The enormous space was totally empty, apart from Paul and the band casually tuning up on a full-size stage located in the centre. There was absolutely no-one else on the floor between the band and myself, some members of the sound crew were standing at the back, preparing for show-time.

Totally curious, I began walking towards the stage, until Paul suddenly spotted me and indicated to his right, towards a small group of people sat at tables to the side. I gave him a quick thumbs-up (as you do) and headed over to find concert promoter Barrie Marshall and wife Jenny (both old friends) with other Marshall Arts' staff.

Also sat there was a small group of besuited, slightly incongruous-looking Japanese businessmen, who turned out to be from tour sponsors Yamaha. After a short while, Paul came and joined us for a quick hello and chat, before being driven back to the stage in a buggy to start the rehearsal a few minutes later.

The run-through was a superb but rather strange experience, as there can't have been more than a dozen of us watching the show, all standing just a few feet in front of the mixing desk at the rear of the arena. It was a full-scale production rehearsal, complete with lights, video backdrop and special effects, plus Paul doing his regular chat between numbers. We remained on our feet for the entire three hours, applauding and enjoying a 35-song set which began with 'Jet' and ended with 'Sgt. Pepper's/The End', a whirlwind trip through Paul's Beatles, Wings and solo careers.

As usual, the last song before the encore was 'Hey Jude', during which the house lights are normally switched on, together with video cameras focussed on the audience as they sing and sway to the long ending. This run-through was no exception, with the 12 of us suddenly appearing on screen as giant figures behind Paul and the band, all of us chanting the familiar *'na na na na'* refrain, with arms held aloft. I know that attending VIP soundchecks is quite commonplace these days, but this was something else.

However, it wasn't quite over yet, as when we returned to the side area for tea, coffee and veggie sandwiches, Paul joined us to ask what we all thought of the show. He was carefully taking in all our comments and seemed totally relaxed after his three-hour stage workout. You don't have to be a mind-reader to know what we told him, while for me this was an extremely rare opportunity to interact with the man himself at close quarters, before and after such a key rehearsal.

Outside 3 Savile Row to celebrate the Blue Plaque, April 28, 2019

CHAPTER 17

HERE, THERE AND EVERYWHERE

I should mention some of the other times I've bumped into Paul and Ringo at various events, or simply just by accident. There have been more than a few, but let's start in September 1982, when Linda McCartney held her first major photo exhibition at the Hamilton Gallery in Mayfair, with a VIP preview held the night before the opening. I was on the guest-list, along with Mike McCartney, Sir Peter Blake, Roger Waters, Chris Farlowe, and others, with Paul and Linda greeting everyone and 'doing the room'. The place was pretty packed, with the wine flowing and canapés (veggie, of course) served throughout.

It was the first time that most people had seen such impressive framed versions of Linda's classic photos of Paul and The Beatles, as well as the Stones, Jimi Hendrix, The Doors, and many more. Also, ordinary people in ordinary situations, as published in the highly-impressive accompanying book, *Photographs*. There were also copies of an attractive exhibition brochure available to pick up, roughly the size of a 45rpm single.

I had the bright idea of asking some of the guests to sign my copy, which Paul and Linda happily did, along with Mike Mac, Sir Peter, and a few others. But did I keep it as a precious souvenir of this special occasion? No, of course not: instead I sent it as a present to Kathy in Minnesota, the girl I met at Aunt Mimi's house the year before. Naturally she was delighted, and I eventually saw it displayed, pride of place, at her home when I visited a couple of years later. Sadly, Kathy died from cancer a few years ago, and I'm not too sure where the original resides now, unless anyone knows otherwise.

In 1990, Paul was presented with the 'Merit Award' at the first-ever *Q* Magazine Awards, the ceremony held at legendary jazz venue Ronnie Scott's in Soho. I received a press invite and arrived rather early, before the lunchtime start. Virtually the only other people there were Paul and Linda, which threw me slightly until I realised that they only had to walk a few yards from the MPL offices in Soho Square to get there.

It was a nice opportunity to chat with them before most guests arrived, until they were inevitably pulled away by others wanting their attention. Compared to (the now defunct) *Q* magazine's much larger ceremonies at other venues in recent years, it was an extremely intimate gathering. Other winners on the day (not all present) included U2 (Best Act in the World); Prince (Songwriter Award); the Rolling Stones (Best Live Act); The Beach Boys (Best Reissue, *Pet Sounds*); They Might Be Giants (Best New Act); and World Party (Best Album, *Goodbye Jumbo*).

In April 1991, I was at London's Savoy Hotel with Richard Buskin, when Linda launched her acclaimed meat-free brand, Linda McCartney's Foods. Linda held our attention as she revealed her pioneering vision for meat-free eating, the start of her mission to try and change people's attitudes towards vegetarianism. She was sitting with Paul at the host table, with Richard and I sat near the back, occasionally exchanging smiles and a few less than reverent one-liners as Paul chipped in to support his wife's extremely worthy cause.

However, despite her best intentions, Linda didn't quite manage to convince either of us non-veggie eaters, so I'm guessing that the two lasses sitting a couple of rows in front of us might have been slightly put out if they'd heard any of our quips. Which may not have been said if we'd realised who they were, but that only became apparent as they stood up afterwards: sorry Mary and Stella, we didn't mean it.

Actually, I did know Mary McCartney slightly. I'd met her a few times on other occasions. She even rang me once, when she was working at MPL for a while, to offer me free tickets for a couple of Paul's 'secret' gigs at the Mean Fiddler in Harlesden and the Cliffs Pavilion in Westcliff-on-Sea. A very focused and classy lady indeed, who of course has since established herself as a celebrated photographer in her own right, as well as being Global Ambassador for Meat Free Monday and Green Monday.

I knew Stella less well but did occasionally see her cycling around St. John's Wood when she was younger, who would always wave if I did. More recently, I was sitting directly in front of her and her family in the VIP section at Paul's O2 Arena show in 2015. It was nice to reconnect, but I could have done without her constant finger and thumb wolf-whistling, which did my ears in for much of the show. Not to mention one of her kids screaming out "Grandude!" half the time.

*

In May 2000, Paul received a special honour from BASCA which was right up my professional street. I've attended almost every Ivor Novello Awards lunch since the early '80s, and for some years was the official researcher for the 'International Songwriter of the Year' award, which always guaranteed me an on-stage namecheck from long-time awards host, broadcaster Paul Gambaccini.

The 'Ivors' are the awards closest to my head, heart and work, as they recognise the best musical creations by the cream of British and Irish songwriters and composers each year, along with special awards to UK and overseas music legends for their outstanding contributions to the industry. The Academy's highest award is its 'Fellowship', which has only been bestowed upon a few distinguished recipients, with the first ceremony of the Noughties being Macca's turn to receive this honour. Other recipients of the award — before and since — include Elton John, Annie Lennox, the Bee Gees, Tim Rice, Andrew Lloyd Webber, Don Black, Joan Armatrading, Kate Bush, and the late John Barry.

Inside the packed-out Grosvenor House Hotel on Mayfair's Park Lane, the lunchtime atmosphere was buzzing with anticipation. Hundreds of music business luminaries, artists and songwriters were in attendance on a sunny May day, which the Ivors always seem blessed with. I was on a table near the front with good friend and former bandmate David Kent, by then an esteemed music lawyer, while sitting directly behind us (practically bum to bum) was Sir Elton John, with a bunch of his management company executives, a particularly noisy lot.

Elton was there to pick up an award for *The Lion King* with Sir Tim Rice, as well as presenting one to the Pet Shop Boys. Other recipients on the day included Robbie Williams, Fran Healy of Travis, Madness, and James Bond composer David Arnold. Plus, over from the USA for the occasion, Jerry Lieber and Mike Stoller, the legendary writers of so many classic hits of the '50s and '60s, honoured for their incredible career.

However, there was mainly one person who everyone wanted to see and pay respect to, no prizes for guessing who. Songwriter and publisher Guy Fletcher was BASCA chairman at the time, and introduced Paul by saying that he had a *"major role in changing the course of British popular music,"* and was *"an exemplary role model for young people the world over."*

Paul walked on stage to tumultuous applause, responding with,

"I remember welling up and thinking, I'm one of them, I'm in that tradition, maybe not like Mozart, but I'm in that tradition. Everyone who's ever had a hit is so proud to be part of it. I'm pleased to be honoured with Lieber and Stoller, Elton, Travis, and the Pet Shop Boys. I remember coming here the very first time with my mates John, George and Ringo and sitting back there, just little kids we were, younger than my kids are now. It was just fantastic to be part of this whole songwriting thing. It was always just the greatest award, the greatest thing to get for songwriters, and it still is many years later."

Indeed, a splendid time was guaranteed and had by all that day. I congratulated Paul very briefly afterwards, but was just delighted to be there, as well as having a small part in the proceedings.

Eight years later, Paul headlined the 2008 Brit Awards at Earl's Court after receiving a special award for his 'Outstanding Contribution to Music' — how many of those has he had? He had earlier revealed that, if the award had been called the 'Lifetime Achievement Award', he would have turned it down, as he obviously knew that he had many more years in him to keep on rocking.

Paul was going through his messy divorce with Heather Mills at the time, which was to eventually cost him dearly, and was clearly going through a rough patch. Luckily, music always wins the day, while he was probably rather pleased at the time in being honoured once again by the music industry. Paul's closing set that night consisted of 'Dance Tonight', 'Live and Let Die', 'Hey Jude', 'Lady Madonna', and 'Get Back'.

There's no doubt that Paul was more than happy to end his rocky marriage by then, despite Heather giving birth to their daughter Beatrice in October 2003. I first met Heather at LIPA Graduation Day that year: she was very friendly but also rather outspoken, with Paul appearing somewhat reserved in her company, I thought. Heather's older brother Shane Mills was working briefly for me at the time, doing some research for *SongLink*. He's also a highly-accomplished musician, whose main instrument is trombone, and whose short-lived instrumental band Dead Singer was extremely dynamic, despite the somewhat unfortunate name.

Paul was on rather more exuberant form later that year, when he brought baby Beatrice to the MPL Christmas party, on his own. I was chatting to friends in the discreet tavern-style restaurant, when Paul suddenly walked in with tiny Beatrice in his arms. He was naturally beaming as he played the proud father, and more than happy to show her off to everyone, along with being full of how much she looked like him, of course. The party was a lot of fun, while I was also pleased to catch up with my sax-playing pal Stewart Curtis, booked with his Klezmer band as the musical turn of the evening.

A few years earlier, Paul was at the Royal Albert Hall for the *Concert for Linda* in April 1999, on the first anniversary of his late wife's death, some 30 years after the couple married, in March 1969. Paul hadn't been expected to perform as he'd done no shows since her passing, but after taking to the stage to thank the audience and a bit of a prompt from co-organiser Chrissie Hynde, he sang one of his and Linda's favourite '50s songs, Ricky Nelson's 'Lonesome Town', backed by The Pretenders and Elvis Costello.

He followed this with 'All My Loving', with most of the evening's performers joining him on stage, before finishing with the inevitable 'Let It Be'. It was a highly moving show, other performers on the night including Tom Jones, Sinead O'Connor, Des'ree, Heather Small, Neil Finn, and Marianne Faithfull.

However, the highlight for me was George Michael performing 'Faith' and two Beatles covers, 'Eleanor Rigby' and 'The Long and Winding Road'. I remember thinking to myself at the time that George could have easily become the nearest British equivalent to Frank Sinatra if he'd wanted to, being such an incredibly gifted and perfectionist singer. Tragically, that was never to be.

*

There have been plenty of McCartney shows I've missed out on over the years, with a couple irking slightly as I could have made them had I been free. For instance, Paul's fundraising lunchtime gig at London's 100 Club in December 2010, which helped save the venue from certain closure. I knew about it and could probably have secured a ticket — if it wasn't for the fact that I was at the Music Publishers' Association Christmas Lunch on the same day. Been to plenty of those but never saw Paul at the 300-capacity 100 Club, my mistake.

Then, during June and July 2018, Paul played a number of small shows to celebrate the launch of his *Egypt Station* album, firstly at the Philharmonic pub in Liverpool, part of his hilarious *Carpool Karaoke* episode with James Corden. This was followed by shows at Abbey Road Studios, LIPA, and the Cavern. It would have been great to have been at Abbey Road as it's so close to home, but on the day of the show I was in Devon, on holiday with my girlfriend Anita. During that afternoon, I received a text from an old pal working at the studios, asking if I'd like to come along to the show. Thanks again, mate, but sorry, no could do.

Talking of missing out, there was one encounter with Paul a few years ago which still amuses me. For years, when staying in London, he would frequent Richoux Café in St. John's Wood, recently demolished to make way for a new branch of Côte restaurants. Paul would sit upstairs, often on his own for a coffee or late breakfast, to ensure that no one would disturb him. It was the same café I often took my Dad to for lunch, as he lived off Abbey Road following my parents' divorce.

On this particular day I arranged to meet a pal for lunch, who suggested the café because (quote), "You never know who you might meet there." John had never seen or met any of The Beatles but was obviously hopeful, so I told him,

"Ok fine, let's meet there at one o'clock."

As usual, I arrived about five minutes early and started walking in through the revolving door — until I suddenly saw that Paul and wife Nancy were coming out at the exact same moment. We had a quick catch-up on the street, mainly talking about LIPA, while I was wondering where John was, as this was one occasion he really shouldn't miss out on. However, after a couple of minutes Paul said,

"Sorry, we've got to go, see you next time," and off they strolled.

I went inside the café and sat down to text John, who just seconds later turned up, completely oblivious to my brief encounter. Which he couldn't quite believe, as you can imagine — yup, it's all in the timing.

Which was also the case when I also bumped into Ringo and Barbara in St. John's Wood not long ago, either shopping or on their way to Paul's place. On that occasion, it was just a quick hello before continuing on our separate ways.

In August 2011, I was invited to an intimate press conference at the Gibson

Guitar Studio, near Soho, where Ringo was unveiling his self-designed 'Knotted Gun' motif for the Non-Violence Foundation. He was urging other musicians to back the campaign, with its aim of trying to put a stop to violence affecting young people. As soon as I raised my hand to ask him a question, Ringo looked at me and said, "I know you!" with a broad smile on his face.

Years earlier, in May 1975, I was at the showroom opening of Ringo or Robin, the furniture and design company, originally formed in 1969 by Ringo with designer Robin Cruikshank. An old friend of mine, Anne, had been given the job as showroom manager, which was rather convenient for me.

Originally located in the Apple building on Savile Row, the firm relocated with Apple to St. James Street, before opening its new showroom on Grosvenor Road, near the river by Vauxhall Bridge. It was situated in premises formerly known as Francis Wharf, inevitably knocked down years later to make way for a block of luxury flats.

Robin Cruikshank had originally been commissioned by Ringo to design a stainless-steel fireplace for him and Maureen in the late '60s. Ringo then started to give Robin some more creative assignments, the two eventually starting work on furniture and other designs. That partnership lasted until 1986, after which Ringo let Robin use the company name and 'star' logo so he could continue trading, as he still does today, in Berkshire.

I recall speaking with Ringo during the party, at which various eye-catching — and highly futuristic — glass and chrome items were on display. These included glass-topped tables, backgammon sets and mirrors, including one designed around a green Apple logo. However, the most celebrated piece was a brilliant chrome-silver coffee table made from two Rolls Royce grilles, which sometime later I also saw on display in Harrods. Fabulous stuff if you can afford it.

A more recent Ringo encounter was at Jerry Lee Lewis's 80th birthday show at the London Palladium, in September 2015, also featuring guitarists Albert Lee and James Burton, among others. Ringo and Barbara were sat in the stalls not far from my aisle seat, so it was easy to say hello before the lights went down. It was an excellent show, with 'the Killer' on good form despite his age and recent ill-health, playing a great set of rock'n'roll classics and country songs. The piece-de-resistance took place at the end, after a storming 'Great Balls of Fire' which had many of the crowd jitterbugging in the aisles. MC Mike Read then introduced Ringo on stage with Robert Plant, along with promoter Rocco Buonvino, all pulling a trolley with a huge birthday cake for Jerry Lee — a nice touch.

Another memorable concert took place in July 2007, when I went to see Steely Dan at Hammersmith Odeon (or the Eventim Apollo, as it's been horribly renamed). I had a perfect front-centre seat, with my friends Vince and Sally also there, but further back. As I turned around to wave to them, just as the lights were going down, my sightline was suddenly averted by two familiar faces sneaking into their seats, just two rows behind mine. Hello, good evening and welcome, Paul McCartney and David Gilmour, nice to see you both. The two superstars obviously enjoyed the outstanding show as much as everyone else, as when I occasionally looked round they were standing and cheering with the rest of us.

In September 2016, Paul and Ringo made a very public appearance together at the world premiere of Ron Howard's feature-length documentary film, *Eight Days A Week* at the Odeon, Leicester Square. I was there with Glen Knowler of the Trembling Wilburys, among others. The two ex-Beatles spoke to press and TV crews for some time outside the cinema before the screening began. Later, as soon as it ended, they were both introduced on stage, to rapturous applause.

Recalling their memories of the Fab Four's touring years, and the film's enhanced soundtrack by Giles Martin, Paul commented,

"Tonight we were actually able to hear ourselves on stage properly for the first time. We couldn't ever hear ourselves when we were live, as there was so much screaming going on."

I thought the film was good, but as many others also realised, it was made mainly with the US market in mind, with scant mention of the many Beatles UK appearances and tours. However, it was great to see the ones that were included, in full HD format, complete with the enhanced soundtrack, which helped to win it a Grammy Award for 'Best Music Film' the following year.

As mentioned earlier, it was rather special to be at the O2 Arena in December 2018, when Paul introduced Ringo on stage to join him on 'Get Back', along with Ronnie Wood. The place went wild as Ringo took to the drum stool to play the iconic train-like shuffle on the Beatles' 1969 hit, and while it was a slightly chaotic version, nobody cared: this was the surviving half of The Beatles, playing live together in London once more.

An historic reunion, especially for the many fans there who quite possibly had never seen either Paul or Ringo playing live in concert before. If that's the last time we see them performing together, then so be it. But somehow I doubt it.

Above left: Sparring with author Richard Buskin during a trip to Peterborough. Above right: Drinking with Mark Lewisohn after Dutch band The Analogues' performance at Abbey Road Studios, June 2019

Left: with the late great Neil Innes of the Bonzo Dog Band and The Rutles.

Below: Author Lesley-Ann Jones with Paul McCartney at LIPA, July 2019. Pictured behind are Tom Robinson and Mark Featherstone-Witty.

Above left: with Freda Kelly and Richard Porter, Leicester Square. 2016.

Above right: With the *Sgt. Pepper* bass drum after it was auctioned at Christie's in 2008.

Left: Julian Lennon holding my signed copy of *Valotte* at AIR Lyndhurst Studios, 1998.

Below left: With Klaus Voormann at Popkomm in Berlin, 2008.

Below right: with Denis Cook and Tony Bramwell in Baker Street for a Blue Plaque unveiling, 2013.

Above left: Paul and Linda McCartney
outside MPL in 1983. *Right*: Olivia and
George Harrison at the premiere of *How
To Get Ahead in Advertising,* 1989.
Left: Cynthia Lennon with third
husband Noel Charles and Bob Harris,
at Abbey Road Studios for Cancer UK's
Sound & Vision, 2009.
Below: Jonathan Clyde, Pattie Boyd and
Jeff Dexter at BBC Maida Vale.

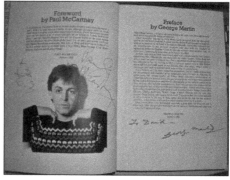

Above left: With my American friend Blaze Reynolds at Abbey Road Studios in the '80s.

Right: my copy of Brian Southall's 1982 book, signed at the launch by Paul, Linda and George Martin.

Left: Sir George, Dave Harries and Ken Townsend at an APRS lunch.

Left and below: Glen Knowler who plays George in the Trembling Wilburys, at Abbey Road Studios for the fiftieth anniversary celebrations of *Sgt. Pepper* in 2017.

Above left: The nearest I've got (as yet) to playing a session at Abbey Road. *Above right:* with the late Geoff Emerick at the Music Producers Guild Awards in 2016.
Left: Maciej Werk from Poland with some of the original Apple Scruffs, at the *Abbey Road* album's fiftieth anniversary celebrations, 2019.
Below: tribute band Fab Gear do the walk exactly, fifty years to the minute since the album cover was shot by Iain Macmillan in 1969.

136

Top: Brother Nigel in our father's Humber Sceptre Mk I (1963), which may or may not be the car driving away on the *Abbey Road* sleeve.

Centre: Fab Gear with Frank Nash's replica of John's psychedelic Rolls Royce. L-R: Merv Johns, Phill Marshall Agourakis, Steve Salvari, David Minchin and Joe Kane.

Right: Fab Gear onstage at the Dublin Castle. L-R: Joe, David & Phill.

Above left: On the roof of 3 Savile Row with Ken Wharfe and Dave Harries, January 30th 2009. *Above right:* Inside the Apple building for Roy Carr's book launch in 1996. *Left:* With legendary US Beatles promoter Sid Bernstein. *Below left:* With Mark Lapidos and Jorie Gracen at the Chicago Fest. *Below right:* Paul at LIPA with Ellie Weinert and Anita Maguire, 2015. Bottom: Outside the Dakota, 1984.

Above left: My niece Mimi Brock-Stark at LIPA with Paul plus Mike Mac behind, 2018. *Above right:* The Beatles hairdresser, Leslie Cavendish with Lesley-Ann Jones.

Left: with hard-working friends and fans Gloria and Steve Holmes of www.Beatlesdays.com. *Below:* Ingrid Black's wonderful cover painting in full. Visit her at www.ingridblack.com to see more of her superb works.

CHAPTER 18

BEATLES FOR SALE

As you may have gathered by now, I'm a bit of a Beatles nut, but as well as having a wealth of personal stories and encounters, I've also attended all sorts of Beatles conventions, auctions, media events and blue plaque unveilings over the years, some of which I've been directly involved with. Not to mention playing drums at a few of the latter celebrations — they didn't nickname me Ringo Stark at school for nothing.

London's first major rock and pop auction took place at Sotheby's in Belgravia on December 22, 1981, catalogued as 'Rock'n'Roll and Advertising Art'. It featured a relatively small collection of lots associated with Elvis, Hendrix and others, the majority of the collection consisting of Beatles items, including two upright pianos: a Steinway owned by John, which sold for £7,000; and a Chappell & Co. model owned by Paul, (his father's before him) which achieved £9,000, rather more than the estimate price of £1,500 - £2,000.

I was at that first auction, and have been to many others over the years, mostly as an observer but occasionally as a buyer. Apart from Sotheby's, the other main auction houses dealing in pop, rock and Beatles memorabilia were Bonhams, Christie's and Phillips, along with a few regional dealers dotted around the country. Today of course, the market has exploded, with rock and pop auctions being held every few months, either here or in the States, and also online.

A couple of London auctions still linger in the memory: firstly, a unique offering at Sotheby's in the mid-'80s for a copy of an Apple Records catalogue from 1971, *The Beatles From Apple: Photos and Biographies*, never officially published. The reason was that this proof copy had John Lennon's scrawly handwriting all over it, inside and out, complete with an extremely explicit instruction on the front cover:

"Who made this shit without showing me? I want it withdrawn immediately. Lennon."

It wasn't hard to see what John disliked about it, as the cover didn't exactly portray The Beatles in their best light. In fact, it didn't portray them at all, as John wrote further:

"Why aren't The Beatles on the cover? Who wants to look at fruit?"

Yup, the red-faced designer thought it would be clever to put a photo of a bunch of apples on the front cover, rather than the four famous faces who owned the company. The other big mistake, which obviously rattled John, was the order of The Beatles' first names included below the photo, listed in alphabetical order rather than in the traditional way. It awkwardly read, 'George, John, Paul, Ringo' instead of John, Paul George, Ringo, to which John had taken his red felt-tip and, with a combination of arrows and numbers, put them in the correct order.

There was plenty more inside the brochure which offended John's sensibilities, as virtually every other photograph — which formed a potted history of the group from early days onwards — featured his sneering scrawl all over, under and sideways around it. An extremely rare and valuable document, and one I would have loved to have purchased if I could have afforded it.

As it happens, I was able to sneak a few photos of some of the pages at the auction preview, as did my good friend Jim Woodley, who managed to take shots of all the pages sporting Lennon's graffiti. The brochure eventually sold for around £20,000 and hasn't been seen in public since, although I believe it was re-sold some years later.

Another memorable auction sale — also involving a Lennon-related item — took place at Christie's in 2008, when my friend and BAFTA-winning TV comedy writer, Gail Renard, sold her unique copy of John's original handwritten lyrics for 'Give Peace A Chance'. John gave them to Gail when she was a 16-year old in 1969, after she gained access to his and Yoko's suite at the Queen Elizabeth Hotel in Montreal, where the Lennons were staging their famous bed-in.

A lady after my own heart, Gail got to know the couple and visited them during the week of their stay, John eventually giving her his draft copy of the lyrics. The reason was that he needed to copy out a much larger version of them for the recording of the song, as famously played in the packed hotel room for the benefit of the world's media. Gail's lyrics sold at Christie's for £421,250 ($833,654), while at the same auction the iconic bass drum head from the *Sgt. Pepper* album cover, designed by Sir Peter Blake, went for £541,250 ($1.07m).

The amount of Beatles memorabilia sold by auction, specialist shops, eBay and other sites, as well as private deals over the past 50 years, is quite staggering. I still find it fascinating to look through the many auction brochures I've collected over the years, and browse the excellent photographs of many of the lots. There have also been a few auctions that took place in tandem with Beatles conventions, with one usually held in Liverpool each year to coincide with International Beatle Week.

*

The first Beatles convention to be held in London (apart from Fan Club meet-ups in the '60s) took place at Alexandra Palace, Muswell Hill, in late December 1976

— the same venue John Lennon attended for the *14 Hour Technicolor Dream* happening in 1967. Billed as 'Europe's First Christmas Beatles Convention', the two-day convention wasn't a great success, with most of the rather thin crowd trying to keep warm in the huge rooms of the unmodernised building, where the BBC were based during the war.

Apart from a number of stalls in the Grand Hall; book signings by Allan Williams, aka *The Man Who Gave The Beatles Away*; and a live performance by vintage Mersey band Faron's Flamingos, there wasn't much else on offer. Apart, that is, for the first 'Beatles Brain of Britain' contest, won by a young chap named Mark Lewisohn, who I didn't know at the time but within a few years would become good friends with.

However, I didn't see anything of the quiz or Faron and his Flamingos, as I was busy manning my own table, selling multiple copies of a book I happened to come across just a few days earlier. I'd been at Claude Gill Books on Oxford Street and noticed a sale display of *The Longest Cocktail Party*, paperback edition, by former Apple insider Richard DiLello. It was originally published in 1973 at £1.90 but now going for a bargain 50p. Taking a risk, I decided to buy every copy, about 40 in total, and took them to Ally Pally, where I priced them up at three pounds each and managed to sell the lot. Typically, they're now worth up to £30 each today.

So that was my main experience of the *'forlorn, dreadful'* event, as later described by former Cavern DJ Bob Wooler, and apart from the entertaining sight of seeing him and Allan Williams getting more and more inebriated together over the day, he was quite accurate. I already knew Allan as he ran an antiques stall most weekends at Dingwalls' market in Camden Town, which I also did for a short time. I was selling sets of colourful Pop Art collages I'd designed and had framed, featuring Marilyn Monroe, Elvis, Groucho Marx and others: anything for a few extra bob back in the '70s.

It was also Wooler and Williams who launched the first 'Liverpool Beatles Convention' at Mr. Pickwick's Club a year later, in 1977. Meanwhile, the 'First Annual Mersey Beatle Extravaganza' was launched at Liverpool's iconic Adelphi Hotel in 1981 by Liz and Jim Hughes, the couple behind Beatles attraction 'Cavern Mecca' on Mathew Street, which ran until 1984.

The Adelphi became the setting for all subsequent conventions from the early '80s onwards, held each August Bank Holiday weekend. I often attended with Richard Buskin, Mark Lewisohn and Mark Cousins, all long-time fans and budding authors, if not yet published at the time. We often had a good giggle about some of the more eccentric-looking fans wandering around the hotel, one particular lunch delicacy on offer also amusing us, the famous Liverpool 'Scouse' stew, not so much for its nourishing ingredients but more for its actual name. Is it still popular, I wonder?

International Beatle Week, as the Liverpool convention is now called, has hosted an extraordinary number of special guests and performers over the years, with Mark Lewisohn becoming one of its most distinguished speakers, especially since *Tune In* was published in 2013. I've met all sorts of Beatle people there, including Pete Best, Klaus Voormann, Freda Kelly, Julia Baird, Pattie and Jenny Boyd, Johnnie Hamp, Joe Flannery, Lee Curtis, and Tony Bramwell, among any others.

Another regular attendee during the '80s was John Lennon's Uncle Charles, brother of his father Alfred, who obviously enjoyed his few hours of fame each year, meeting fans and signing autographs. He died in 2002, aged 83, while many more familiar names in The Beatles' remarkable history have also since passed on. Not so surprising really, as 2020 marked an astonishing 60 years since the name 'Beatles' was first coined.

I've also attended the American 'Fest for Beatles Fans' in Chicago a few times these last few years, usually en route to other locations in the USA. In 2012, it was good to catch up with a couple of 'Scotts', namely ex-Abbey Road engineer/producer Ken Scott and US musician Tom Scott, whom I'd last met with George Harrison outside Capital Radio in 1974. I was also a guest speaker of Jorie Gracen, editor of the *Macca Report,* who interviewed me about a few of my Beatle encounters and LIPA. I was back in Chicago in 2015 but saw rather less of the Fest proceedings this time due to the following anecdote, which you may or may not find amusing.

I flew in from London with Anita, on the first day of the festival, but on a very tight schedule as we were due to catch an early flight to Nashville the next morning to visit my step-sister Liz and family in nearby Pulaski, TN.

We arrived in Chicago during the afternoon and checked into the Marriott Hotel at the airport, where the Fest is held. A short while later we went down to meet Richard Buskin, who now lives in Chicago, as well as Mark Lewisohn, who had also flown over for the convention. The four of us sat down for an early supper and a catch-up, during which I suddenly began to feel rather queasy in the tummy department.

Not to be put off by this, Anita and I went to a late afternoon panel session, featuring no less than 13 Beatles book authors, all seated in a row on stage to plug their latest offerings, including Richard.

We sat in the front row as the session commenced, each speaker talking about their book in turn. However, I didn't get to see more than a couple of them, as within a few minutes I suddenly felt violently sick, making a rush for the side door to find a men's room as quickly as possible. Unfortunately, I didn't quite make it in time. Instead, one of the PA speaker stands by the stage was the unlucky recipient of my early supper, in full view of a room full of incredulous fans.

I was helped out of the room to recover in the service area, spending the rest of the evening upstairs in bed. However, by around 11 o'clock I was feeling a lot better, so I ventured back down to catch the final hour of the day's programme.

This happened to be a talk by Fest founder Mark Lapidos, holding court in a darkened hall to relate the history of the event and how, in New York during the '70s, he'd met John Lennon, who turned out to be something of a Beatles fan himself. This inspired Mark to launch the Fest, which used to be held three times a year in different locations (now twice). As we had to leave early the next morning, that was practically all I saw of that year's event. Yes, totally nuts.

*

During the summer of 2003, I was invited to play drums in a new tribute band being formed, the John Lennon Experience, featuring Gary Gibson, who looked and sounded uncannily like John. Gary previously achieved some fame by appearing as Lennon on popular ITV programme *Stars In Their Eyes* during the '80s, and for years fronted his own group, Cavern, based in the North-West of England.

Our new band featured a great bunch of musicians, including lead guitarist John Brosnan, a good pal who has since performed as George Harrison in many bands, as well as in the long-running *Let It Be* stage show. Phil Mann was originally on bass before P.J. Phillips took over; Andy Hamilton on saxophone; and Matty on keyboards, the line-up completed by Jo and Jules, our two gorgeous female backing vocalists.

After much rehearsing, the band gelled extremely well together, with the aim of playing the kind of show that John might have given if he'd gone on tour in 1981, as originally planned. So, plenty of solo songs, including a few from *Double Fantasy* and *Milk and Honey,* along with Beatles classics like 'Come Together', 'Don't Let Me Down' and 'Revolution'.

Our first show was — where else? — in Finland, for around 2,000 people at the annual 'Back to the Sixties' weekender, in a fabulous winter resort named Katinkulta. The reason for this being that organiser Ande Päiväläinen, who played drums for top Finnish '60s band The Strangers, was a good pal of mine, and loved the idea of us debuting at the festival.

The show proved to be a massive success, and was televised locally – you can see a great clip of '(Just Like) Starting Over' on YouTube which has had thousands of hits. I'm just pleased that I got the short but tricky drum-break near the end of the song absolutely spot-on, especially for our first performance. It was great to get such good audience reaction, and I have to confess that playing drums behind Gary did spookily give me the occasional feeling that I was playing with John for a second.

From there, we went on to play a club in Helsinki, also booked by Ande, with other shows scheduled by band manager Rocco Buonvino. Back in London, we played the legendary 100 Club on Oxford Street to great acclaim, the first time I'd played there since the '70s. The venue has hardly changed at all over the years, and until Coronavirus hit, I was still going there on a semi-regular basis. Meanwhile, the next big JLE gig was in early 2004, at the Olympia Theatre in Paris, as part of a major show to celebrate 40 years since The Beatles had played no less than 18 dates there in early 1964.

It was a fantastic experience, as apart from L'Olympia being the nearest French equivalent of the London Palladium, the concert was totally sold out and a huge success. It also featured Tony Sheridan (of the Beat-Brothers and 'My Bonnie' fame), as well as a full orchestra backing a local tribute band. We closed the first half, with Gary wowing the crowd, the backstage area afterwards totally chaotic as so many people were coming up to congratulate us. It was also great to meet Tony and share the stage with him, a very nice guy who sadly died nine years later.

We also played at a Dutch Beatles convention to mark the 40th anniversary of the group playing two shows in Blokker, a small town north of Amsterdam. This was the setting for the Fab Four's only shows in Holland, in June 1964, albeit with Jimmie Nicol replacing the absent Ringo, famously hospitalised in London, having his tonsils removed. Ironically, Gary couldn't make our gig either, so we had a 'dep' John with us named Paul (!). He was very good indeed, but it wasn't quite the same.

Not long after that, the band disbanded, a great shame as in my humble opinion we were the best-ever Lennon tribute. Not least because of Gary's looks and voice, plus our full-on sound, enhanced by the girls' fab backing vocals, and Andy's brilliant sax-playing helping nail our arrangements of such numbers as 'New York City' and 'Whatever Gets You Through the Night'. We all put a lot of effort into the band, so it was a great shame that we didn't stay together longer, for geographical and other reasons   .

However, every cloud has a silver lining if you put your mind to it, and I'd had an idea for a while, which I now had time to fulfil. This was to organise a 30th anniversary reunion of my old band Riviera Feedback, who last played together in 1976, a few months after our show at the Marquee. I'd jammed or played with the guys at parties a few times over the years, but thought we should try and get back together as I still loved our original songs, mainly written by Dave Kent.

It took a while, but we eventually began rehearsing, which went well, so I booked a couple of shows. The first was on the Battersea Barge, near Vauxhall, a Thames-side bar and music venue owned by friends; while the second show took place at Corks Wine Bar off Oxford Street, just before Christmas 2006. Both were great fun and well attended. I'm extremely pleased that we played them and spent time together, as not long afterwards Dave was diagnosed with pancreatic cancer, sadly passing away in October 2007, aged just 54.

This was a huge loss, especially as I'd known him from school since the age of 11, while, as mentioned, he eventually became a top music lawyer, greatly respected in the industry. A few years later, lead guitarist Richard Rangeley also left the stage, from lymphoma in 2011. Another tragedy, for as well as being a totally affable chap and great friend — despite being late for virtually every single rehearsal and gig — he was also one of the best axemen on the planet, or at least in north London.

My next band venture evolved in 2009, from playing Sunday afternoon jam sessions at The Castle pub on Finchley Road, near Hampstead. The pub had been transformed into a highly stylish venue by Denis Cook, also a great singer and musician in his own right, who now lives and performs on the Costa del Sol. We played all sorts of rock, pop and blues covers, while one Sunday a chap dressed all in black and wearing shades came up to me to say,

"I can sing just like Roy Orbison if you know any of his numbers?"

Well, we did, and he could, so Dave Collison became a regular performer with us at the jam sessions. This was especially fortuitous for me, as apart from loving Orbison's music I also knew the Big O's widow, Barbara Orbison, very well indeed through my work, as she ran his record and publishing companies from offices in Nashville.

I briefly met Barbara and Roy Orbison for the first time ahead of his last-ever performance in Europe, at the Diamond Awards in Antwerp in November 1988. It was there that he gave his only public rendition of 'You Got It' (co-written with Jeff Lynne and Tom Petty), suddenly dying of a heart attack back home in Tennessee just 17 days later, aged only 52. Another great loss to the music world, especially as the *Traveling Wilburys Vol. 1* album had only just been released.

So, we were playing a bunch of 'Big O' songs, among other covers, with Dave Collison doing a great job as Roy, but had no thought of taking it further. That is until I went along to an English Heritage Blue Plaque unveiling at 34 Montagu Square, just off London's Baker Street. This was the apartment where John and Yoko lived for three months in 1968, sub-let from Ringo Starr, who previously let it out to Paul McCartney and Jimi Hendrix on different occasions. The plaque dedication to John Lennon in October 2010 was a big deal, as Yoko Ono was there in person to unveil it, while the flat was (and still is) owned by a friend of mine, Reynold D'Silva of Silva Screen Records, who even offered it to me as a rental a few years ago. Maybe I should have moved in.

I was standing in the crowd, waiting for Yoko to arrive and for the ceremony to begin, when I suddenly noticed someone standing a few feet away who bore a remarkable resemblance to George Harrison. I walked over to him, chatted and asked if he was a singer or musician. He introduced himself as Glen Knowler and said yes, he'd done a bit of performing over the years but not much recently.

I mentioned the band to him and asked if he'd fancy coming down one Sunday to try a few numbers with us, which not long after he did. The line-up of what eventually became known as the Trembling Wilburys was complete.

We then had a lot of hard work cut out in rehearsing over the next few months, with a large repertoire of songs to learn from the Traveling Wilburys' catalogue, plus some of their solo hits. Apart from the two frontmen, the other band members are Andy McNish on guitar (as both Bob Dylan and Tom Petty); Marko Laver on bass (as Jeff Lynne); Dzal Martin on lead guitar; Howard Robin on keyboards; plus yours truly as session drummer Jim Keltner, aka 'Buster Sideman'.

Dzal has played with Terry Reid, Box of Frogs featuring Jeff Beck and Jimmy Page, Meatloaf, and many others, as well as being a long-time member of The Equals, of 'Baby Come Back' fame. Meanwhile, I've played or jammed with Denny Laine, Randy Bachman, Earl Slick, Dave Berry, Mike Berry, The Quarrymen (of which more shortly), the late Jim Diamond, and others along the way — we have pedigree, you know.

Hard to believe that was 10 years ago, but since then we've played a huge amount of shows around the country and abroad. Most of our work has been in London and the South-East, but we've travelled as far afield as such exotic places as Butlin's in Skegness, other holiday camps in Hayling Island and Great Yarmouth, 'Beatles Days' in Mons, Belgium, Ludlow in Shropshire (co-headlining with Marty Wilde), plus many other places. And, inevitably, we made it to the Cavern Club in Liverpool, where we shared a bill with Steve Rodgers (son of Paul) and his excellent band in 2017, as well as on other occasions with them. I just hope we can return to the Cavern one of these days.

It's a lot of fun playing the best of the Traveling Wilburys, as well as solo numbers by the five members of that brilliant super-group. Sadly, only two of them are still with us today — Bob and Jeff — so we feel it's important to keep the Wilburys' flag flying and give the kind of show they might have played if they'd ever toured together. Plus, everyone loves the songs and the great fun vibe the band generates.

Our shows usually start with a first set consisting of solo numbers, from Orbison's 'Only The Lonely' and 'Oh, Pretty Woman' to George's 'Here Comes The Sun' and 'Something'; and from Dylan's 'If Not For You' and 'I'll Be Your Baby Tonight' to Petty's 'I Won't Back Down' and ELO's 'Hold On Tight', among many others.

The second set usually kicks off with 'She's My Baby' and 'Dirty World', continuing with such Wilburys classics as 'Last Night', 'Rattled' and 'Tweeter and the Monkey Man'. We invariably end with 'End of the Line' and 'Handle With Care', before slamming into rocking encores of 'Runaway' and 'Roll Over Beethoven', the latter performed as a mash-up of the Chuck Berry, Beatles and ELO versions. There's plenty of other great tunes in the sets, so please check us out on Facebook or at our website, www.tremblingwilburys.co.uk

CHAPTER 19

FOR YOU BLUE

A mong the many shows the Trembling Wilburys have played are a few which have celebrated the unveilings of various showbiz Blue Plaques, usually in honour of distinguished celebrities who have passed on. We pretty much became the house band for the 'Heritage Foundation', an organisation founded by the late David Graham, who hired us on many occasions to play at his regular Blue Plaque lunches.

He originally launched the organisation as the 'Dead Comics Society', with the erection of a plaque in 1991 for Peter Sellers at his old home in Highgate, while over the years since many other stars of stage, screen and music have been honoured. I was a regular attendee at many of the Blue Plaque unveilings, usually followed by glitzy luncheons at the Regent's Park Marriott Hotel in Swiss Cottage, a very handy location for me.

One of the first we played was in 2013, at a luncheon in honour of John Lennon and George Harrison, their joint Blue Plaque put up at the old Apple building on Baker Street. Glen Knowler and I attended the unveiling along with Rod Davis of The Quarrymen, Rick Wakeman, Tony Bramwell, and others, before heading back to the Marriott for the lunch and speeches. The event concluded with our finale set of Beatles, Wilburys and Orbison songs, getting many of the guests on the dancefloor — despite constant complaints from Her Majesty The Queen, actually an elderly actress, that we were much too loud. Sorry, your Maj, tough shit.

We also played at similar tributes to Bernard Cribbins, Lionel Blair and the late Jeremy Lloyd (the latter two having both appeared in *A Hard Day's Night*); John Altman, of *EastEnders fame*; the late Roger Lloyd Pack (Trigger in *Only Fools And Horses*) and others. Every event saw the function room occupied by many showbiz celebrities, whom we were delighted to entertain as well as meet, from June Whitfield and Leslie Phillips to Liz Frazer and P.J. Proby, with many more in between.

One group of elderly gentlemen invited on a regular basis were RAF veterans from Bomber Command, the celebrated World War II squadron which became the pet charity of the Heritage Foundation. It was always a great honour to see those brave ex-servicemen, in their late '80s and '90s at the time, inevitably given a standing ovation by everyone in the room. The substantial donations to their fund — not just from the luncheons — eventually led to the construction of the imposing Bomber Command Memorial at Hyde Park Corner, officially unveiled by the real HM Queen Elizabeth II in June 2012.

*

Two years later, there was one particular Blue Plaque idea I was keen on initiating, and eventually ended up organising from start to finish. Early in 2014, I'd read a newspaper article detailing how a proposal for a memorial plaque to Brian Epstein had been turned down by English Heritage, not for the first time. The proposer was Geoffrey Ellis, Brian's former right-hand man at NEMS Enterprises, who lived close to Epstein's former home at 24 Chapel Street in swish Belgravia.

By coincidence, Ellis was head of the legal department of Dick James Music at the same time I worked there, some 40 years earlier, so I had a somewhat tenuous connection. I gave him a call, explaining that I had a plan which might be a good alternative to his failed attempt in getting English Heritage to accept his proposal. He expressed interest, so I arranged to meet him at his smart flat on Eaton Place.

From 1965 to 1967, Geoffrey Ellis ran the London offices of NEMS as Chief Executive, based at Sutherland House, located next door to the London Palladium on Argyll Street. I suggested to him that this would be the (second) best place to erect a plaque for Brian. After giving the matter some thought, he eventually agreed. Geoffrey was extremely pleased that I'd taken such an interest in his quest, while also rather bitter that English Heritage had snubbed his well-intentioned proposal, which he thought was quite ridiculous of them.

I told him that I'd look into it and find out who actually owned Sutherland House, as the permission of the freeholder is always required to put up a plaque or change any aspect of a building's exterior. As it happened, this turned out to be a lot easier than I expected, as an online search quickly led me to discover the owners. I contacted their managing agent, who had no idea whatsoever that the offices had any previous association with Brian Epstein or The Beatles but promised he would check whether my proposal would be acceptable to his clients.

To my surprise, he got back to me extremely quickly, to inform me that it was indeed acceptable, and that permission had been granted in principle. We were allowed to erect a Blue Plaque on the building, providing it didn't cost the freeholders or cause any public inconvenience on the day of its unveiling.

This was excellent news indeed, which not only delighted Geoffrey Ellis but also David Graham, as it would mean another prestigious Heritage Foundation plaque unveiling, followed by a celebrity lunch at the Marriott. I subsequently had the unenviable job of selecting and inviting many of the VIP guests for both the ceremony and the lunch — always a juggling act, as invariably there are a few who aren't available to attend on an allotted date.

Eventually, after weeks of planning, the unveiling was set for noon on Sunday June 29, 2014. The plaque was erected the previous day and covered up until Sunday morning, when a blue velvet curtain was placed over it. I was down there early to supervise and because I'd arranged for the restaurant on the ground floor to open especially early, so coffee and croissants could be served to the VIPs as they arrived. This worked out very well indeed, many guests turning up in eager anticipation of the big event, as well as getting a free brunch.

A sizeable crowd had also gathered on Argyll Street, along with press and TV crews, so just before noon I stepped outside with Geoffrey Ellis; actress Vicki Michelle (chair of the Heritage Foundation); actor Andrew Lancel (who played Epstein in the eponymous play); and Adam Ant, whose Mum had been Paul McCartney's cleaner during the '60s (about as tenuous a connection as you can get, but I knew Adam). I spoke a few words to explain how the plaque came about, before Vicki and Geoffrey gave their speeches. Then, together, we pulled the blue cord to drop the curtain and reveal the Blue Plaque, which simply stated,

"Brian Epstein managed The Beatles and other artists from offices here 1964-67".

The wording had to be short and meaningful in order to read, as the plaque was placed rather high up on the first floor of the building. If you're ever at Oxford Circus or visiting the London Palladium, just look up above what is now a branch of Five Guys burger restaurants and you'll see it there.

Other names who joined us at the ceremony included Tony Bramwell, Rod Davis, Tony Crane of The Merseybeats, authors Bill Harry, Mark Lewisohn, Lesley-Ann Jones and Richard Porter (of London Beatles Walks), film producer Martin Lewis, radio presenter Eric Hall (ex-EMI) and songwriter Mitch Murray CBE, among others, as well as two of Brian's London-based cousins. I had hoped Cilla Black would be joining us, but a few days earlier her son and manager Robert Willis messaged me to say that regretfully she wouldn't be able to make it, a great shame. Sadly, Cilla died just over a year later, after a fall at her villa in Estepona, Spain, aged just 72.

After the ceremony ended and various media interviews were concluded, we all headed to Swiss Cottage, where coincidentally Brian Epstein had lived when he first moved to London as a drama student. Lunch at the Marriott was a highly celebratory occasion, with many more Heritage regulars attending who hadn't made the unveiling, including journalist David Wigg, who interviewed The Beatles many times for the *Daily Express* during the 1960s and beyond.

More speeches were made by Geoffrey Ellis, Bill Harry, Tony Bramwell, Martin Lewis, Vicki Michelle and myself, who also had the job of reading out messages from some of those who couldn't make it on the day. These included Brian's former secretary Joanne Petersen, who now lives in Australia; author and former Beatles PR man Tony Barrow; Cilla, Gerry Marsden, Ringo, and this from Paul:

"I know Brian would have been very proud to think that he had earned a Blue Plaque in the West End of London. He played a very important role in guiding the early career of us Beatles, and more than that he was a lovely man whose friendship we all valued, and who I will always remember with great fondness. Congratulations Brian. Love from Paul McCartney."

After lunch, the regular charity auction and raffle included various framed items bearing Brian's image, which all raised good amounts, while as usual the event was rounded off by the Trembling Wilburys. Although I was slightly drooping after such a long day, as soon as I sat down at the drums the adrenalin kicked in. I felt proud to have orchestrated the whole proceedings, with thanks to Geoffrey Ellis's original idea. Brian Epstein would have turned 80 on September 19, 2014, while Geoffrey passed away four years later in 2018, aged 87.

*

Five years on, I was back on the Blue Plaque trail again, but this time with three other companions, our aim being to honour a highly significant date in The Beatles' timeline: January 30, 1969, when the group performed for the final time, on the roof of their Apple building in Savile Row. An historic occasion indeed, which for years many fans had hoped would be marked in some form at the famous building — still a popular tourist attraction with the fans — but on this occasion it took a lot more groundwork to achieve.

I can't claim any credit for instigating the idea, as local property agent David Rosen, who still works on Savile Row, had made it a personal mission of his for a long time, before bringing in his film-maker friend Mark 'Bax' Baxter; Beatles tour guide Richard Porter; and myself to help make it a reality.

David has been in the property business for so long that he actually sold 3 Savile Row for Apple in 1976, and still has the documentation to prove it. He's also a big Beatles and music fan, who has some nice ephemera in his office, while Bax has made films about Sir Peter Blake, The Jam, and jazzman Tubby Hayes, whose memorial plaque in Soho he also helped with. Richard is the founder of London Beatles Walks and co-author of recent book *The Beatles in Liverpool, London and Hamburg*, and used to own the Beatles Coffee Shop at St. John's Wood tube station, now renamed Helter Skelter.

Our small but ambitious team — instantly nicknamed as the other 'Fab Four' — had its work cut out, as the main reason no plaque had ever been put up at 3 Savile Row, despite previous attempts, was the fact that it's a Grade 2 listed building. This means that any application not only had to be approved by the building's freeholders, but also by Westminster Council, involving some extremely complicated paperwork. The reason for the building's listing was that, since its construction in 1733, it had been occupied by the Duke of Wellington; Admiral Lord Nelson's mistress Lady Hamilton; and other historical dignitaries, much later belonging to entertainment impresario Jack Hylton.

Fortunately, we had no problem with the current leaseholders, retailers Abercrombie & Fitch, whose children's clothes shop occupied the building at the time. David Rosen received permission for the erection of a plaque from the building's freeholders, so the only remaining hurdle was to convince Westminster Council that they should also approve it. This took much longer than expected, at least six months from when we first grouped together in the summer of 2018. We were hoping to have obtained permission by the end of that year, so the plaque would ideally be unveiled on the actual 50th anniversary of the rooftop concert, January 30, 2019 — well, that was the plan anyway.

I should also mention here architect Tom Croft, an associate of David Rosen's, who kindly agreed to help us with the final stages of submitting the application, which had to be absolutely precise in technical terms. By coincidence, Tom's firm previously worked on a building for Paul McCartney, while his professional input into our comparatively tiny project was to prove absolutely vital.

To our slight consternation, we missed the actual anniversary, but it didn't really matter, as we were eventually given the final go-ahead by Westminster a few weeks later, cause for a small celebration in David's office.

Finally, a small Blue Plaque ceremony took place on the morning of Friday April 5, 2019, at the rather early hour of eight o'clock. It was held then for various reasons, not least because it was one hour before the shop's opening time, but also to avoid pedestrian or traffic disruption. Unfortunately, I wasn't too well that day so sadly missed it all; a shame but just one of those things. However, my three colleagues were all present, joined by actor Bill Nighy, *GQ* editor Dylan Jones and a few others on the steps of the building.

The one thing that hadn't been granted was access to the famous roof, which would have been the icing on the cake, but proved a definite no-go area. Luckily, I'd already been up there a couple of times, as Richard has, including for the 40th anniversary of the concert in 2009, when the interior of the building was in a state of demolition. A small group of us were carefully led upstairs by the property developer in a hard-hat, along with a two-man camera crew from CNN International, there to interview former policeman Ken Wharfe — later bodyguard to Princess Diana, but a rookie cop in 1969 who can be seen in the *Let It Be* film — and ex-EMI engineer Dave Harries. You can see my personal video of them both on YouTube, while bizarrely the American CNN cameraman bore a remarkable resemblance to Billy Preston.

The previous time I'd been up on the roof was for the press launch of former *NME* editor Roy Carr's book, *Beatles at the Movies - Scenes from a Career*, published in 1996. I went along with brother Nigel to enjoy the drinks and nibbles served on the top floor. Everyone present (including Jarvis Cocker for some reason) was given free access to the roof during the course of the evening, although not all at the same time for obvious reasons. It was fascinating to be up there, and be able to walk around the extremely small area The Beatles had played on that cold January day in 1969.

Following the early-morning Blue Plaque ceremony, a much bigger celebration was held outside 3 Savile Row on Sunday April 28, with a great turnout. Attendees included Beatles roadie Kevin Harrington; Apple driver John Mears; *Let It Be* cameraman Paul Bond; Dave Harries; ex-AIR Studios manager Malcolm Atkin; singer and photographer Debi Doss; office worker Sidney Ruback, who made it up to the roof in 1969; four of the original Apple Scruffs; session legend Mo Foster, plus Beatles authors Barry Miles and Tony Barrell, among others. In addition, live music was provided by Hiran de Silva and David Minchin, who busked a bunch of Beatles songs — just as they had on the actual anniversary in January. So all in all, a fantastic outcome which the alternative 'Fab Four' are all extremely proud of.

*

Speaking of busking, there's another Beatles-related show I was proud to have been part of, when two of the Trembling Wilburys became honorary members of The Quarrymen for one night only. This happened at a rare London appearance by the group at St. James Theatre in Victoria, now owned by Andrew Lloyd-Webber and since renamed 'The Other Palace'. The reason for the show was to celebrate the London opening of a play about John Lennon, *And in the End*, written by award-winning American playwright Sandy Marshall.

I'd received a call a few weeks earlier from Quarrymen frontman Rod Davis, who I know well, to say that their long-time original drummer Colin Hanton — who had never missed any gigs before —needed to have an operation on his shoulder, so could I step in for him, along with a bass player in place of Chas Newby? This was a real no-brainer, so fellow Wilbury Marko Laver and I duly turned up on May 6, 2013, both dressed in typical Quarrymen-style check shirts and looking forward to playing with the guys.

Despite having no rehearsal — we were truly busking it — the show went extremely well, with much positive feedback. It even made the *Evening Standard* the next day, with a photo of us. For one night only, the veteran band— originally formed by John Lennon in 1956 — consisted of Rod Davis on acoustic guitar and vocals; Len Garry also on guitar; John 'Duff' Lowe on piano; plus Marko and myself.

We really got into the swing of it, as did quite a few audience members, whom Rod traditionally asks up on stage to play washboard on a few numbers. These included 'Puttin' On The Style', the old Lonnie Donegan song that the group played at St. Peter's Church Fete in Woolton, Liverpool on July 6, 1957, the day that John famously met Paul for the first time (although Paul has now confirmed that he originally saw John on a bus before then, and also in a Garston chippie).

Other songs we played included 'The One After 909', 'In Spite of All the Danger', 'That'll Be The Day', and a heartfelt version of 'In My Life' sung by Rod. It was a total pleasure to be performing with the very guys who played in the group which eventually became The Beatles: I even stripped down my large Pearl drum-kit to basics for the occasion, and made a 'Quarrymen' logo for the bass drum head.

It hasn't happened again since, as Colin's thankfully been in good health, with the band still playing a few gigs each year (up to 2020) in the UK and abroad. Incidentally, Rod has joined the Trembling Wilburys on a couple of occasions, when we've played informal acoustic sets at the 'Beatles Days' collectors' markets in London, run by our good friends Steve and Gloria Holmes. Thanks again Rod, always a pleasure to do business with you.

CHAPTER 20

ALL TOGETHER NOW

At this point I'd like to namecheck some of the other notable Beatle people whom I've encountered over the years, either related to the group or who had extremely close personal or working relationships with them. This is by no means a definitive list, just a round-up of a few names that I may not have mentioned elsewhere on these pages.

I met **Cynthia** and **Julian Lennon** on various occasions, including at Abbey Road Studios, when Cynthia attended Cancer Research's annual *Sound & Vision* fund-raising event a couple of times. She was with her fourth husband, Noel Charles, who originally came from Barbados, and who was keen to inform me that he had promoted a couple of northern club gigs by Jimi Hendrix back in the '60s. I initially found Cynthia to be slightly reserved, not unexpectedly as I didn't know her that well, but as soon as I mentioned that I'd known Mimi, as well as meeting John a few times, she became much more at ease. I had huge respect for her over the years for retaining her dignity, despite having suffered the extremely public degradation of John replacing her with Yoko in 1968.

Cynthia was a lovely lady who raised Julian on her own extremely well: I'm sure that his being the focus of her life, especially after his father's death, helped give her the strength to deal with her own personal circumstances, which were often far from easy. By coincidence, another friend of mine at *Sound & Vision* in 2010 was Barbara Orbison, Roy's widow, with whom Cynthia got on very well. I took a memorable photo of the pair of them standing below portraits of their respective late husbands, as displayed on a Studio 2 wall prior to the dinner and charity auction. Sadly, Barbara died just over a year later in December 2011 from pancreatic cancer, while Cynthia also died from cancer at her home in Majorca on April 1, 2015.

I can't claim to know Julian that well, but I did spend some time with him at AIR Studios in 1998, when he was promoting *Photograph Smile*; an album I thought was very good but unfortunately remained under the radar. I told him about my connections with his father and great-aunt, which he was extremely interested to hear about, and asked him to pose for the camera holding my copy of his first album *Valotte*. He's also played and recorded with a few mutual musician pals, including Matt Backer, Martyn Swain and Guy Pratt, while for some years he was signed to Hit & Run Music Publishing, co-owned by Genesis manager Tony Smith with Jon Crawley, another old pal. I've seen Julian play live a few times and hope he might return to the stage again sometime, as he has some good songs which don't often get heard these days.

*

I first met **Olivia Harrison** in 2005, at Traffic drummer and songwriter Jim Capaldi's funeral in Marlow, by the River Thames. Like me, Olivia is friends with Jim's widow Aninha, whose daughter Tabitha worked in the UK music industry before moving to her mother's native Brazil. I happened to be queueing for the buffet meal with Olivia and son Dhani at the wake in the Capaldi house; we actually thought we'd met somewhere before but couldn't quite think where.

The next occasion was in 2011, at a branch of Waterstones bookshop in Piccadilly, when Olivia was there to sign copies of her book *Living in the Material World*. I went along with Glen Knowler, aka George Harrison of the Trembling Wilburys, who was rather nervous of how Olivia might react to meeting such a close lookalike of her late husband. However, she didn't mind at all, despite an initial look of surprise. I mentioned to her that a clip of George and Pattie walking past me at the *Yellow Submarine* premiere had been included in the *Living in the Material World* documentary film, directed by Martin Scorsese. Olivia replied,

"Yes, I remember that bit, we especially included it in the film," which was nice to know. Look out De Niro and Pacino, you have serious competition on your hands.

The most recent time I met Olivia was in June 2017, at an evening to celebrate publication of the expanded edition of George's autobiography *I Me Mine*, originally published by Genesis in 1980. It was a superb event in Covent Garden, also attended by Jeff Lynne, Eric Idle, Terry Gilliam, Jools Holland, Annie Nightingale, Damon Hill, and others.

I was there with PR guru Judy Totton, who was also at Jim Capaldi's funeral, and has known Olivia a long time, as she took the photos at Joe Brown's second wedding in 2000, when George was his best man. However, on this occasion it was me taking a snap of Olivia and Judy together, standing by some of the many examples of George's original hand-written lyrics on display in the gallery.

*

I've bumped into **Zak Starkey** on many occasions, being a fellow drummer who used to hire the same west London rehearsal studio as my band over the years. He's a nice guy and a great player, who as well as having Ringo for a Dad was also encouraged to play drums by Keith Moon, who gave him a kit for his eighth birthday. Being a huge Who fan myself, I've seen him play with them loads, although not quite as many times as I saw Moonie on stage. Zak's been doing a terrific job for the last couple of decades, while he's also played with Ringo's All-Starr Band, Oasis, the Icicle Works, John Entwistle, the Lightning Seeds, and Johnny Marr and the Healers.

In 2009, I arranged for The Who's former tour manager John 'Wiggy' Woolf's long-forgotten hologram of Keith Moon to be put on display at a special Heritage Foundation luncheon. This was to celebrate the unveiling of a Blue Plaque for Moonie in Wardour Street, close to where the Marquee Club was famously located.

The primitive early hologram had only been seen in public once before, at the band's 'Who's Who' exhibition at the ICA in 1978. I was also there, and had never forgotten the striking light-design. More than 30 years later, the spooky green 3-D laser image of Keith perched at his kit was almost hidden in the Grosvenor House Hotel, as it had to be covered by a canopy of black curtains in order to view it properly. I managed to take a photo of Zak and Kenney Jones posing in front of 'Keith', a very rare shot of the main three Who drummers all pictured together.

*

Klaus Voormann famously met The Beatles in Hamburg during the early 1960s, maintaining his relationship with them right through their career and beyond. As well as designing the brilliant artwork for *Revolver* and *The Beatles Anthology*, he also played bass for Lennon, Harrison and Starr on various albums, as well as being a member of the Plastic Ono Band. According to the *Daily Mirror*'s dramatic headline in April 1970, he was set to replace Paul McCartney as *'the new Beatle'*, which was news to him and everyone else.

I met Klaus in Berlin in October 2008, when he gave a talk at the annual Popkomm music industry exhibition (no longer running), which coincided with a spectacular one-man exhibition, entitled *Remember Revolver*. This was dedicated to his artwork, and also the launch of a custom Volkswagen Beetle inspired by the album. He'd designed the eye-catching VW coachwork with images from the 1966 record sleeve, with many more of his framed works on display in the multi-storey gallery, Beatles music playing continuously. I made a short video of the event, using 'Tomorrow Never Knows' as the soundtrack, which was up on YouTube for more than 10 years, before I received notification that it had been taken down due to copyright infringement, the rotten spoilsports.

I next met Klaus in late August 2018, when he was in London to promote his latest book and exhibition, *It Started in Hamburg*, with a special media luncheon. This was held during the launch of the 'Hamburg on Tour' exhibition at Brick Lane in the East End, which featured promotions by many of the city's tourist companies. Klaus was there in collaboration with Stefanie Hempel, founder and guide of the 'St. Pauli Beatles Tour' of Hamburg, and a very talented singer/songwriter in her own right. I've been on her tour and she does a fantastic job.

Klaus surprised us all by playing acoustic guitar, and briefly duetting with Stefanie on an impromptu version of 'Something', witnessed by just a few people in her booth but I'm glad that I was one of them. I subsequently sat with him during the lunch, provided for more than 20 media folk, during which he was extremely talkative and happy to sign the book and other items. A genuinely nice and super-talented guy, who has his own special place in The Beatles' history, and whose fantastic artwork, books, designs and creativity will surely be acknowledged for many decades to come.

*

I've known **Bill Harry** since the 1970s, and have always been extremely impressed by his extensive work as a prolific writer, editor, PR man, broadcaster and commentator on The Beatles. Of course, Bill was one of the very first to write about them in *Mersey Beat*, the music paper he launched in Liverpool in July 1961, with the exhaustive number of books he's worked on over the past 40 years and more quite mind-boggling — just check his Wikipedia entry for all the titles, around 30 in all.

The one I've probably referred to most over the years is *The Beatles Encyclopaedia* (Virgin, 2000), which does exactly what it says on the tin, being a superb 'who's who' of Beatle people, with Bill probably knowing them all as well.

He's always been a lovely guy to meet and deal with, plus he's kept the legacy of the Mersey Sound going with his exhaustive web archives at www.triumphpc.com. As previously mentioned, Bill and I both received our BASCA Gold Badge Awards in October 1995. I was delighted to sit next to him — and Larry Adler — for the group photograph taken that day.

*

Tony Bramwell has been a pal for the past couple of decades, although I didn't know him during his Beatles, NEMS or Apple days. However, our paths must have crossed at some point in the late '60s, especially when he was promoting the Sunday-night Saville Theatre shows for NEMS, which I only wish I'd been able to attend more of. We first met properly after he picked up the rights to Eva Cassidy's hugely-successful posthumous album *Songbird* for indie label Hot Records, the late American singer's stunning voice and recordings becoming a radio phenomenon after Terry Wogan championed her on BBC Radio 2.

Since then we've met up at all sorts of events, from Beatles conventions and Blue Plaque unveilings to the MIDEM exhibition in Cannes; the BBC Club; and various other notable watering holes. What I especially like about Tony is his complete modesty, keeping his illustrious career with the Fab Four extremely quiet, never mentioning what he achieved with them, especially on Facebook. But seriously, anyone who hasn't read his great book *Magical Mystery Tours: My Life With The Beatles* should do, as it's full of great anecdotes and useful information, from one of the real insiders who grew up with the group.

*

Like Tony, **Leslie Cavendish**, aka 'The Beatles Hairdresser', has also written an excellent book, *The Cutting Edge*, which has sold extremely well since publication in 2018. Although we're from the same area of north-west London, we only met a few years ago at a Pizza Express jazz evening in Soho, but have since become good friends. Leslie originally hails from Burnt Oak near Edgware, with his late uncle being Tony Crombie, a celebrated British jazz drummer, whose son Russell was a friend of mine during the late '60s and early '70s.

Leslie has been busy promoting his book over the past couple of years, appearing at Beatles conventions, on cruises and online, while we've attended various gigs and sports events together. He's also seen the Trembling Wilburys in action a few times. There are some hilarious 'hair-raising' stories in his book, especially when in 1969 he inadvertently implied in the press that John Lennon might start losing his hair before any of the other Beatles — check it out if you haven't already done so.

*

Alistair Taylor was assistant to Brian Epstein at NEMS, and the person who went with him to see The Beatles at the Cavern for the first time on November 9, 1961. He subsequently became the group's 'Mr Fixit' during their hectic touring years, devising escape routes from venues; helping to resolve copyright issues and assisting them with property purchases, among other duties. I got to know him much later, during the 1980s and '90s, when he was semi-retired but managing a band named Smoke. We had a few positive meetings about them, but unfortunately they didn't hit the big time. A genial character who usually liked to meet in a pub, I eventually lost touch with him, while Alistair sadly died from bronchial problems in 2004.

*

Sam Leech was a Liverpool concert promoter during the early '60s, who staged more than 40 Beatles shows between 1961 and 1962, as well as putting on artists like Jerry Lee Lewis and Little Richard at such venues as New Brighton's Tower Ballroom. He later devoted his life to the history of Merseybeat, speaking about his career at conventions in the UK and overseas.

In October 2015, I visited him at his modest Liverpool home, with my good pal Randy Bachman (of Bachman Turner Overdrive) and Jeff Parry, producer of the *Let It Be* stage show, which was opening in Liverpool that same week. Sam was delighted to meet us and relate some of his many stories, and also show us various replica posters of some of the concerts he'd promoted back in the day.

He wasn't in great health, and was pretty much house-bound, but it was a pleasure to meet him and listen to his memories, all recalled with a wicked sense of humour — along with his insistence of how integral his role was to the pre-fab Beatles and other groups. He died from cancer a little over a year later, in December 2016, with Jon Keats of Cavern City Tours commenting at the time,

"It's sad news as we've lost another part of the Cavern's and Liverpool's history. Sam was a key part of the early years of The Beatles and put on many of their shows in Liverpool before they hit the big time."

*

Last but not least, **Pete Shotton** was John Lennon's boyhood pal at Dovedale Infants School and Quarry Bank Grammar, and an original member of The Quarrymen, playing washboard until Paul McCartney joined the band. He maintained his friendship and links with John and The Beatles right through their career, eventually serving as manager of the Apple Boutique, and also as the first managing director of Apple Corps for a short while. He also ran a supermarket on Hayling Island, off the south coast of England near Portsmouth, which John bought for him during the '60s, before successfully developing a chain of American-style diners, Fatty Arbuckle's, in the 1980s.

I only met Pete once, following publication of his excellent autobiography, *John Lennon: In My Life,* in 1983, but it's an interesting story. I travelled to Hayling Island to interview him for *The Beatles Book* monthly, having been commissioned and subsequently paid by editor 'Johnny Dean', aka Sean O'Mahony. However, the interview was never published, as O'Mahony objected to the use of a swear word Pete had used at the end of it — a shame, as it could easily have been edited out. What follows is my original planned introduction to the article, along with some of Pete's responses to my questions.

On the frontispiece of 'John Lennon In His Own Write', published in 1964, there is a caricature by John of a curly-haired fellow with strange-looking

birds perched on his head and arms. It's a fetching little drawing of no real significance to anyone in particular, except for one person, for whom it is an affectionate reminder of the closeness, humour and companionship between two old chums.

Exactly 20 years later, the curly-haired fellow depicted in that picture has decided to tell the story of his friendship with John Lennon for the first time, from the day when they first met in Sunday school aged six to their final get-together in New York 30 years later.

The story is told in a book just published, entitled 'John Lennon In My Life' by Pete Shotton with Nicholas Schaffner, and in this, his first ever interview for a British magazine, I asked Pete to talk freely, starting with the significance of the number nine in John's life.

"He never made a specially big thing about his birthday at all, not during the '60s. He didn't even think about Christmas as anything out of the ordinary," said Pete. "It was, if you want to celebrate or you want to have a party, you can do it anytime. So he never made a big thing about Christmas or his birthday. Number nine just happened to be his lucky number, and green was his favourite colour.

"I think he put more importance on things after he met Yoko, his attitude changed considerably and he became more concerned, like that instance of him writing that note to you (via *Disc* in 1969). He started communicating with a lot of people just to say thank you. Pre-Yoko, he was very blasé about everyone, but after that he started appreciating people more, maybe because he felt that what he was doing was more important. He became pretty prolific in note and card writing.

"What happened with Yoko was that he acquired an entirely different set of fans who appreciated John during this John & Yoko period. I think, if I may say so, that a lot more 'intelligent' people became interested in him. I think that people of importance were taking more notice of him, as they realised that this was no longer a cuddly long-haired mop-top Beatle, this was an intelligent man who was thinking and being active, and in a way was a yardstick to a lot of people, even if they didn't exactly go along with what he did.

"People related to him on a very personal level, it wasn't like it was when it was with The Beatles, apart from the later years when he was coming through into what he became after Yoko. He was a pop star who was famous and rich and all those things, but there was something more important, people felt that they had contact with him personally. He had that level of communication which was very unique, as well as keeping his feet firmly on the ground, without letting any of that crap getting to him.

"The last time I saw or spoke to John was in October 1976: we said we've got to keep in touch with each other and should start writing, but we never did. He was a conscious part of my life because he was involved in it for so long. He was an enormous part of it, through all the stages of it really. As little kids, as teenagers, all the memories of a great part of my life involved John. And he also helped me financially of course. I actually finish paying back the loan next year *(1984)*.

"In 1980 it was my wife who phoned me as she'd gone out early to work and heard the news on the radio. I immediately called George's house, but he was still asleep. They hadn't woken him up to tell him, which was a bit of a surprise. So then I drove up there to see him, we talked and then Ringo called from the States and he spoke with him. We all sat round the table, as George had a session booked for that day in his house. The musicians started arriving, so I asked him what he was going to do, go on with the session?

"He just said, 'Yes, what else is there to do, we've just got to get on with it.' He was very calm about it, although his inner feelings must have been in turmoil. He was very philosophical, because George is a very spiritual person, and as he said, which I'd forgotten about, just pray for John and think of him because although he's been blasted out of his body he's still there, he's OK, he's just moved on, you know. So that was his attitude to life, we're only passing through here, and you know that this is nothing to do with what we really are.

"My reaction was a bit different: I was totally stunned and shocked, not too pleased about it at all really. In a way it's a daft question, when someone that close to you has died, especially in that way. I think everybody felt anger without a doubt, anger at the insanity of it.

"And the last line of the book says it all. It was the day that we were taking it into the publishers, we had the manuscript finished, but Nick (Schaffner) couldn't do the ending, he'd been thinking about it for months. On that morning I woke up before Nick did and went down to his apartment. I got a cappuccino on the way and then tried his door, but the key wouldn't turn. It was pissing down with rain, but I knew he didn't have to get up until 10:30 as he'd only gone to bed at seven, so I thought, I'm not going to wake him up just to let me in.

"So I just stood outside, and for some reason started whistling 'Ob La Di, Ob La Da', which is a song that I never liked anyway. But for some reason I just started whistling and singing it. At the same time it was on my mind that we still hadn't got a conclusive ending to the book.

"So, I'm there humming and whistling 'Ob la di, life goes on', and I just thought well, that's it. It served a double purpose, as it was a song that John didn't like either — by the same token 'Ob la di' says it all because life does go on, we must all remember that. I mean don't dwell on his death, you've got to remember his life, so it just came to me there and then.

"I then rang the doorbell and found I'd just turned the key the wrong way, even though I'd been in his flat dozens of times, it was unbelievable. So I went in and told Nick, who said,

'You know all day yesterday you were singing 'Ob La Di'.

I then told the whole story to him, I thought that was the best thing I could do, and at the end of it I just said, 'Well, what a fucking ending, eh!'

"So then I just said, 'That's got to be it, that's got to be the last line of the book, in its own right. When I turn that last page over, I want to see that right on the final page: 'What a fucking ending', and that's how it came about."

CHAPTER 21

AND IN THE END

The year 2019 proved to be another landmark for The Beatles, in as much as it saw *Abbey Road* returning to the top of the UK album charts for its 50th anniversary. It also happens to be my favourite album of theirs, while the multiple celebrations taking place that summer and autumn included some highly notable events to tie in with it.

The first, and biggest, was the gathering of hundreds of fans outside Abbey Road Studios to mark 50 years since the front (and back) cover photograph of the album was taken, from up a step-ladder by Iain Macmillan on August 8, 1969. The anniversary has been celebrated outside the studios for the last 20-odd years by Richard Porter of London Beatles Walks, but the 2019 event drew the largest attendance to date.

Thanks to great weather, and the fact that the traditional mass walk across the zebra crossing — 50 years to the minute — had been well-publicised, it was a huge story. By 11 o'clock, Abbey Road was completely blocked off, as fans caused major disruption to cars, buses, taxis and even police vehicles for at least an hour or more. The chaos was also helped by a special ingredient added to the mix, with the arrival of tribute band Fab Gear, especially put together for the occasion.

The previous year, Richard had booked the band from the *Let It Be* stage show to turn up and do the traditional walk. However, for the 50th anniversary he wanted to do something a bit more special. He had the inspired idea of the walk being followed by a special afternoon gig at the Dublin Castle pub in Camden Town, an iconic local venue where the Trembling Wilburys had played just a few months earlier.

He originally asked if I could play drums, which I was all set to do until I had a problem in both my hands, caused by carpal tunnel syndrome (luckily all okay now). So I couldn't play, which was just as well as I look nothing like Ringo, but did help to put the band together. I started with suggesting the excellent Phill Marshall Agourakis as John Lennon, having both known him from the annual 'Beatles 1 Day' held in Twickenham each May.

Phil loved the idea and was quickly followed by Joe Kane from Scotland as Paul, then by David Minchin from Hamburg as George. Richard and I both knew David, as he had busked outside 3 Savile Row in January for the 50th anniversary of the rooftop show with Hiran de Silva. However, the drum stool was still vacant, despite my asking a few good 'Ringos', none of whom were available for the fast-looming date. But as luck would have it, just two days before the gig, David Minchin — who's Australian — mentioned that his old bandmate Mervin Johns was up for it and was all set to fly over from Perth to play the show. Quite extraordinary news.

Merv and his wife Simone arrived in London just in time for the solitary rehearsal that I'd organised for the night before the gig, at Westbourne Studios off Harrow Road, which the Wilburys and my other bands have been using for years. It's a great rehearsal complex, which as mentioned Zak Starkey also used when he lived in the area. Always a Beatles connection.

I also had the idea for one extra band member to join the group for the show, which I knew would work well — except that initially, this friend and occasional bandmate of mine wasn't too sure if he could actually make it, as he had his own album launch booked for that very same evening at a top venue in the West End.

Thankfully though, he eventually agreed, so enter Billy Preston, in the shape of keyboard player Steve Salvari, formerly of '80s funk band Circle Line, who has both the look and musical ability of the late great American keyboard player. Of course, Billy Preston was the only person to be famously credited as an artist on a Beatles single ('Get Back') apart from the group themselves.

Luckily, Steve is also a huge Beatles fan, who really didn't want to miss out on this once-in-a-lifetime opportunity. The single rehearsal went very well, all of us leaving the studio pretty late, despite having an early start the following morning. We arranged to meet up by St. John's Wood tube station, as a special mode of transport had been arranged by Richard to drive the band the short distance to Abbey Road Studios and the famous zebra crossing — that's a crosswalk for US readers.

That mode of transport was — big drum roll — a perfect replica of John Lennon's famous psychedelic Roll Royce Phantom V, owned by Frank Nash in Essex and used for high-end Beatles tours in grand style. When the incredibly eye-catching car eventually arrived at the crossing, complete with its suitably-dressed occupants, after carefully navigating the huge crowd of fans in the way, the response to the four 'Beatles plus Billy' jumping out of it was just amazing.

It was just like Beatlemania of old times, with everyone cheering and waving, trying to see the band up close and taking photos, causing a massive crush. It was a totally bonkers experience, with many photographers and TV crews also getting in on the action. Eventually, the fab foursome managed to walk over the crossing a few times, posing to get it just right for some superb press shots, as used all over the world, before moving on to the Dublin Castle.

The afternoon gig was also a huge success, the pub totally packed out with a terrific atmosphere, thanks also to the '60s discs spun by DJ and venue booker,

Tony Gleed. The guys all played and sang brilliantly, with Steve, aka 'Billy', also getting into it, so much so that one or two people thought he really was the late Mr. Preston. Most bizarre.

A few other performers joined in for the inevitable, if slightly chaotic, finale of 'Hey Jude' and other numbers, along with yours truly banging my tambourine, despite wearing splints on both hands. I was highly relieved and most impressed that drummer Merv had flown in, all the way from Australia, as not only did he play brilliantly, but totally looked the part, and is a very nice guy indeed. Thanks again Merv.

Thus, the *Abbey Road* album cover-shoot was well and truly celebrated in grand style, which couldn't possibly be matched by the 50th anniversary of the album's actual release date, a few weeks later on September 26. Apple and Universal Records had certainly pulled out all the stops to push the album back up to No. 1, with huge press, radio and TV coverage. Meanwhile, BBC Radio 2 devoted a large chunk of its output that week to The Beatles, with all sorts of features and interviews, as well as a special digital pop-up station devoted to the group.

There was a large media crowd gathered outside the studios during the morning of the anniversary, but not many there when I popped down at lunchtime to take a quick look round. Later on, Paul and Ringo turned up for a private party at the studios, with friends such as Olivia Harrison, Nile Rogers, Sir Patrick Stewart, Martin Freeman, and also *Rocketman*'s lead actor, Taron Egerton. My invite must have got lost in the post.

Another celebratory event worth mentioning was Dutch band The Analogues' incredible recreation of the entire *Abbey Road* album, held in Studio 1 earlier in the summer. While not quite a tribute band per se, they are all the most meticulous musicians and vocalists, who strive to perfectly recreate every single note and sound on a Beatles record, even to the extent of playing exact copies of the original instruments used wherever possible. I'd previously seen them at the London Palladium performing the *White Album,* which was also superb, but to see them up close at Abbey Road Studios with near-perfect sound and a huge array of period instruments and gear was something very special indeed.

Indeed, we had Ringo's distinctive anvil-bashing on 'Maxwell's Silver Hammer', and various synthesisers recreating the Moog sounds on 'Something', 'Here Comes The Sun' and 'I Want You (She's So Heavy)', complete with white noise. Plus, an excellent string section on all the tracks which required it, along with great vocals by the various singers.

The performance finished with a terrific version of 'The End' (plus 'Her Majesty' of course), before we all trooped into Studio 2, where the band played on with an encore of earlier Beatles songs. Big thanks to my old plugger pal Judd Lander for sorting passes for us: Judd's a Scouse music legend who fronted '60s band The Hideaways, known for playing more times at The Cavern than The

Beatles did. Plus, he also famously played harmonica on 'Karma Chameleon' and other tracks for Culture Club.

The Analogues were introduced on stage by the world's No.1 Beatles authority, Mark Lewisohn, who gave a short introduction on the history of the *Abbey Road* album before the band came on. In fact, this turned out to be a sneak preview of Mark's forthcoming project, a full UK theatre tour dedicated to him talking about the album, billed under the mysterious title of 'Hornsey Road'.

This was actually a reference to a long-forgotten 1960s plan by EMI Records to purchase premises on Hornsey Road in north London, converting them into studios exclusively for the use of the company's pop roster, presumably including The Beatles. However, this project was abandoned almost as soon as it started, so no wonder the curious name initially baffled many people who bought tickets for the tour.

I went to a couple of intimate previews of the show, and to Mark's appearance at the Bloomsbury Theatre in London, on September 28. He did a brilliant job in explaining how the album was put together, revealing a treasure-trove of previously unknown facts, along with many rare audio and video clips. Who knew that there was an actual 'Mean Mr. Mustard', who really was a miserly Scottish skinflint; or that John was keen to do another Beatles album and Christmas single, despite privately announcing plans to leave the group in September 1969.

One small detail that Mark didn't mention — as there's no proof of it whatsoever — was the possibility that a light-blue car, pictured driving away near the top of the *Abbey Road* sleeve, could have been our Dad's Humber Sceptre Mk 1 1963 saloon (Reg no: AMC 840A), as he lived on Abercorn Place just off Abbey Road after our parents divorced. I've included a photo of it with Nigel in the drivers' seat taken years later, and while it's never been confirmed whether it really is the car on the cover, we both like to think it was.

*

That was all in 2019, but as I write now in September 2020 the world has become a very different place indeed. Hopefully by the time this book is published, the global pandemic will have subsided, but that could still be some time away if predictions are correct. I'm lucky to be able to work from home, as I have been doing for years, but sadly I've lost at least one good friend to the virus — RIP pop quiz maestro Larry Foster — along with a few others I've known in the music business and beyond.

Most gigs and festivals have been cancelled or postponed, while, like thousands of other musicians around the world, I can't wait to get back to eventually playing in front of an audience with my bandmates and others. If we actually manage to do so before the end of 2020 it will be a bonus, but I'm not holding my breath.

It's been such a desperately hard time for live music and the arts, plus its many associated industries, affecting the livelihoods of hundreds of thousands of workers.

There was also a major charity event due to be held at Abbey Road Studios in March 2020, which had to be cancelled during the first week of lockdown. I'm on the organising committee for Cancer Research UK's afore-mentioned *Sound & Vision* fundraising event, which has been held at the studios since 2006.

Sound & Vision's patron and founder was Sir George Martin, along with DJ and presenter Bob Harris, with the 2020 event being planned as a Beatles special. Giles Martin was set to be guest-speaking, along with performances by Texas, Jack Savoretti, and others, with some superb items donated for the auction and raffle. The exclusive dinner has now been rescheduled for 2021 (fingers crossed), and will hopefully match or better the previous event's tally of nearly half a million pounds raised for the charity.

Meanwhile, LIPA's annual Graduation Day ceremony, normally held in late July each year, was also postponed until 2021, a great shame indeed for the class of 2020. The 2019 event was a particularly memorable one, with Paul on great form and more than happy to mingle with guests at the VIP reception afterwards.

These included songwriter/composer and chief Womble, Mike Batt; actor and author Stephen Fry; and Mr. Bean himself, aka Rowan Atkinson, all inducted as new Companions of LIPA, among others. My guest for the occasion was author Lesley-Ann Jones, writer of many acclaimed music biographies, including her latest, *Who Killed John Lennon?,* which I've also contributed to. It's sure to be a bestseller, as were her previous works on David Bowie, Freddie Mercury and Marc Bolan.

In fact, Lesley-Ann mentioned to me that meeting Paul at LIPA was the 'second-best day of my life', after having her three children, which was a lovely thing to say. I have to agree, as it's always been extremely special for me to meet Paul, along with John, George and Ringo over the years — although sneaking into the London Pavilion in 1968 and sitting behind them all does rather take some beating.

Having spent a lifetime observing The Beatles from near and far, and having had some remarkable encounters along the way, it's true to repeat that they were always my main influence, as I told Paul and all the other guests at LIPA in 2006. I only wish my parents had still been alive to share that brilliant day with me, but sadly Mum died from Alzheimer's' and pneumonia in 2003, while Dad passed away a couple of years later, both having been in care homes. I'm sure they would both have been so proud.

Luckily though, Nigel and his partner Karen were both with me at the ceremony, with a memorable shot of the two Stark brothers taken afterwards with Paul, who's giving an appropriate double 'thumbs-up' for the occasion.

Incidentally, at Graduation Day in 2018, I introduced Paul to my niece Mimi Brock-Stark, who later began working for Judd Lander PR, and is now fully involved with the music industry, just like her uncle David. I'm extremely proud of her and of my professional association with LIPA, which I sincerely hope will continue to thrive over the next few years and decades, as it fully deserves to do.

As mentioned at the beginning, it all started with a song — 'Please Please Me' in my case — as it always has been, and still is for me, about that unique body of songs and recordings created by The Beatles, from 1962 to 1969. I've seen shows and enjoyed music by hundreds of other amazing artists and bands since then, in all musical genres, but there's no disputing that John, Paul, George and Ringo wrote and recorded the most influential, melodic and enduring music catalogue of our generation, and hopefully of many generations to come.

The Beatles weren't gods or saints, they were just four talented Liverpool lads, who each did their 10,000 hours of work before making it big, playing sweaty rock'n'roll in Liverpool and Hamburg clubs during those pre-Fab days.

They were also fortunate to have just the right chemistry and dedication; personalities and humour; vocal and songwriting abilities — plus a highly astute manager in Brian Epstein — to take them right to the top. It's very easy to take them for granted these days, but the many career highs The Beatles achieved during their relatively short existence still seem quite remarkable, from 'Love Me Do' in 1962 to 'Let It Be' in 1970, and everything in between. Long may they reign.

I hope you've enjoyed the ride. I know I have.

David Stark with Ben Champniss,
singer of 'Gold Songs' by Fab Gear

GOLD SONGS

Recorded by FAB GEAR

Ben Champniss • Dzal Martin • Phil Nelson • David Stark

Remember all those years ago when yesterday was born
And golden slumbers kissed your eyes while sexy Sadie snored
Oh, life was so much easier, the Walrus kept us warm
A splendid time was guaranteed for all

Chorus:
So play those gold songs, the ones we loved the best
Those old songs, they'll always stand the test of time
Those melodies will always be a part of you, a part of me
The memories they gave us will never disappear

And in a time when love was all and flowers were in your hair
We all enjoyed the Hendersons at Pablo Fanque's Fair
And even though the orchestra has left the bandstand bare
The music still surrounds us everywhere

(Chorus)

Entertaining, celebrating, meditating years
The greatest show on earth for all to hear

And now it's been so many years since yesterday was born
When golden slumbers kissed your eyes while sexy Sadie snored
And though the dream is over and the dreamer's eyes are sealed
We can't forget the songs that made it real

(Chorus)

So play those old songs, those gold songs
Play those gold songs

Music & Lyrics: David Stark
Copyright © 2009 – 2020 Definitive Songs Ltd. All rights reserved.

Watch on YouTube
Search for Fab Gear – 'Gold Songs'

ACKNOWLEDGMENTS

This book has been a long time coming, with many friends and colleagues over the years asking me if I was ever going to write one. I finally began it during 2018, but was forced to stop a few months later due to some health issues, which have luckily all been resolved. It was only when lockdown started in March 2020 that I continued where I'd left off, so I suppose that, in a bizarre way, I must first thank the cursed virus for enforcing a somewhat quieter lifestyle than I'm used to, which gave me more time to reflect and continue to write.

I know that many others have also been in the same boat, taking advantage of suddenly having the extra time to work on creative ideas and projects which they'd put off for years. So good luck with yours if you fall into that category, while my sincere gratitude goes to a few key people who have all made important contributions to the book you've just read.

Firstly, big thanks to Richard Buskin and Lesley Ann-Jones for their forewords, your kind words are very much appreciated. I've known Richard for 40 years and LAJ for slightly less, both being highly-experienced and respected authors in their own right, with a wealth of best-selling books between them. Your ongoing support has been very much appreciated.

Thank also to my brother, Nigel Stark, who actually has a much better memory than mine for events in our early lives, right down to the smallest details. I'm always amazed when he tells me some trivial fact about what we did as kids, saying, "You must remember that," which I often don't — quite remarkable, especially as he's two and a half years younger than me. I must also mention our late Mum and Dad for always being there for us, and taking us to see The Beatles at Hammersmith Odeon in 1965, when I was just 12 and Nigel only nine. We're both eternally grateful that we had the chance to see them play live on stage at least once.

Others who have contributed to this book in one way or another include Chris Charlesworth, for his introduction to Neil Cossar of This Day In Music Books; Patrick Humphries for his continued encouragement over the last few years; Paul Endacott for the front cover layout; Paul Levett for lunch last week; and Mark Lewisohn for being a good pal, whose tireless documenting of the Fab Four is indeed the 'stuff of legend' *(Leggy Mountbatten, 1924)*. Plus, Anita Maguire for her tolerance and some early editorial input; my editors and proof-readers Georgia Melaris and Malcolm Wyatt; designer Gary Bishop; Judy Totton for her consummate PR skills; and Richard Porter, Linda Watts and Jim Woodley for providing photos, sorry if not all of them made the final cut.

Special thanks must also go to Ingrid Black in Montreal, whose wonderful front cover portrait of The Beatles (actually titled *Magical Mystery Tour*) was a huge motivation to me in getting this book finished. As soon as I saw it, quite randomly online, I knew that it was the perfect image to use. It's a totally stunning piece of art, as are many of her other works. I hope to meet Ingrid in person one day and hopefully see the original painting.

Finally, huge thanks and respect to John, Paul, George and Ringo, without whom, etc. The book says it all but yes my friends, I have indeed enjoyed the show, and hope to continue doing so for a long while yet.

David Stark
London NW3
September 2020

PHOTO CREDITS

All photographs © David Stark, unless otherwise indicated below. Every effort has been made to contact the rights holders of any other images which appear in this book. If you have a proprietary interest in any such image please contact the author or the publisher.

OPPOSITE CONTENTS: The Beatles in Knole Park, 1967
© Pictorial Press Ltd / Alamy.com

PHOTO SECTION 1
Page 40: The Beatles at Another Christmas Show, 1964
© Trinity Mirror / Mirrorpix / Alamy.com
Page 41: George Harrison at the Yellow Submarine premiere, 1968
© Leslie Bryce / The Beatles Book Photo Library
Page 41: The audience at the Yellow Submarine premiere, 1968
© Harry Myers / Shutterstock
Page 42: John Lennon outside Marylebone Magistrates Court, 1968
© Keystone-France / Getty Images
Page 42: The Rolling Stones Rock And Roll Circus, 1968
© Trinity Mirror / Mirrorpix / Alamy.com
Page 43: The Beatles Book cover logo
© The Beatles Book Photo Library.
Page 44: John and Yoko at the Magic Christian premiere, 1969
© Hulton Archive / Shutterstock
Page 46: John and Yoko at Selfridges, 1971
© Trinity Mirror / Mirrorpix / Alamy.com
Page 46: Dick and Stephen James, by courtesy of Stephen James

PHOTO SECTION 2
Page 91: 'Companions of LIPA' with Paul McCartney, 2006
© LIPA, Liverpool
Page 94: The Trembling Wilburys
© Christina Jansen Photography.

PHOTO SECTION 3
Page 132: Paul and Linda McCartney
© Richard Porter
Page 133: Olivia and George Harrison
© Richard Porter
Page 135: Fab Gear crossing Abbey Road, 2019
© Reuters / Alamy.com

ABOUT THE AUTHOR

David Stark grew up in north-west London, attending Haberdashers' Aske's School in Elstree before working for Premier Drums, Dick James Music, Decca Records, MAM, and Music & Media/Billboard magazine, among other companies. He was editor of *Sound Engineer & Producer,* the *Producers' Handbook and the Eurofile Directory*, while since 1993 has been editor and publisher of *SongLink International* and *Cuesheet.*

A lifelong musician, occasional songwriter and producer, David also plays drums with the Trembling Wilburys tribute band, who he also manages. He is the recipient of a BASCA Gold Badge Award for his contribution to the music industry, and was made a Companion of LIPA in Liverpool by Sir Paul McCartney in 2006.

A keen quiz fan as well as a Beatles one, David has been on the winning team at the *Mojo Inquisition,* while his *SongLink Saboteurs* have won the Nordoff Robbins Music Industry Pop Quiz three times in the past few years. He lives in Belsize Park NW3, and listens to PopMaster on Ken Bruce's BBC Radio 2 show most weekday mornings.

For further information:
e-mail: david@songlink.com

www.itsalltoomuch.net
www.songlink.com
www.cuesheet.net
Facebook.com/songlink
Instagram: davidstark9611
Twitter.com/songlink

Index

© *PictureLux / The Hollywood Archive / Alamy.com*